VISUAL PERCEPTION

HERSCHEL W. LEIBOWITZ

The Pennsylvania State University

VISUAL

PERCEPTION

The Macmillan Company
Collier-Macmillan Limited, London

Fifth Printing, 1969

Library of Congress catalog card number: 65–20182

THE MACMILLAN COMPANY
COLLIER–MACMILLAN CANADA, LTD., TORONTO, ONTARIO

Printed in the United States of America

Foreword

"The Critical Issues in Psychology Series," paperback source books for the undergraduate in psychology, are designed to provide authoritative and provocative reviews of selected topics germane to a spectrum of courses. Each volume offers an original inquiry into major facets of the point at issue and a set of illuminating reports carefully chosen to represent salient positions of historical or current significance. This combination will afford instructor and student opportunity to read stimulating, even challenging, argument with primary sources in hand.

Visual perception is perhaps the oldest of all psychological problems in terms of historical treatment. How man perceives the world is not only of fundamental importance to behavior theory but also extremely interesting in its own right. *Visual Perception* provides an up-to-date interpretation of the representative theoretical and experimental issues involved and, in so doing, treats the processes involved in normal perception.

Herschel W. Leibowitz, a leader in visual perception experimentation, has long been actively engaged in a variety of research and instructional endeavors concerning the problems of visual perception. Now professor of psychology at The Pennsylvania State University, he has taught at the Universities of Wisconsin and Michigan and at M.I.T. and was recently Manager, Behavioral Sciences, at the IBM Research Center, in this capacity advising engineers on applied perceptual problems as well as basic theoretical issues.

MELVIN H. MARX, *General Editor*

Preface

IT IS CUSTOMARY, WHEN INTRODUCING A NEW TOPIC, TO begin by attempting to define the problem at hand. In the case of visual perception, this task could conceivably take us back to the history of philosophy and the origins of psychology within philosophy, physiology, and physics. Such a journey, although intellectually stimulating, might prove to be unsatisfactory, because a universally agreed-upon definition of perception simply does not exist, and any attempt to formulate a satisfactory definition would merely result in elaborations of the problem and reasons for failure. On the other hand, all of us are aware of the world around us. We see objects, colors, sizes, shapes, faces; hear sounds; taste food; and smell odors. In a less rigorous sense, a working definition of perception can be considered as an awareness of our environment. Such a simple definition will suffice to initiate a discussion of this fascinating and important topic.

One of the reasons why a definition is so difficult to obtain is that this field cuts across and is part of many other disciplines. The student of art, the engineer, the physician, and the psychologist, to name but a few, are all interested in perception. The perceptual literature is richer for having received contributions from astronauts, observers of children and animals, zoologists, and poets. In a sense, the diversifications and ramifications of perception are at the same time both a liability and an asset. The liability consists of the necessity, although not a critical one, for a wide range of background information before the material can be well understood. In addition, a concise definition is not available.

On the positive side, the many aspects of perception, its application to various phases of life, and its ubiquity all add to its inherent interest. The broadness of the field requires contact with a wide variety of disciplines, so that one is gently led to a broad point of view with desirable consequences.

As with most topics, and particularly in perception, it would be possible, although not practical, to attempt a comprehensive and complete coverage of all aspects and facets of the problem. In the case of perception, it would be desirable to include, among others, its anatomical, photochemical, medical, historical, philosophical, aesthetic, educational, and engineering aspects. This approach, although having the virtue of scholarship, is not feasible in a work of this size and is certain to be incomplete and perhaps even unfruitful. As an alternative, it is proposed to select eight aspects of visual perception that are thought to be important as well as representative topics of study in this field. Unfortunately, other aspects will be passed over. The value of the selective approach is, hopefully, both to stimulate interest in this field and to leave the reader with an awareness of *some* fundamental problems and facts of the area of perception. If the reader is left with a feeling of interest and perhaps even excitement, despite an inevitable sense of incompleteness, this goal will have been attained.

It is assumed that the reader will have some previous familiarity with the field of general psychology inasmuch as the present topics are elaborations of general psychology with special emphasis on the problems of perception. The material on adaptive aspects, innate factors, learning, attention, motivation, illusions, and the role of the nervous system in perception are classic topics in general psychology. The chapter on the role of perception in modern technology has not yet achieved such "classical" status but is rapidly moving in this direction. It is hoped that the study of perception within this context will give the reader not only a broader appreciation of perception itself, but will also contribute to a deeper understanding of this aspect of general psychology.

HERSCHEL W. LEIBOWITZ

Acknowledgments

Preliminary work on this volume was initiated in the summer of 1963 during the author's tenure as visiting professor in the Department of Psychology, Massachusetts Institute of Technology, under the auspices of grant NsG 496 from the Behavioral Biology Program, National Aeronautics and Space Administration, to the Psychophysiology Laboratory at M.I.T. The continuing encouragement of Professor Hans Lukas Teuber of M.I.T. is deeply appreciated.

The material presented here has developed with the help of research support extending over a period of 13 years conducted at the University of Wisconsin, the University of Munich, the Max Planck Institut für Verhaltensphysiologie, the University of Michigan, International Business Machines Corporation, and the Pennsylvania State University. During the major portion of this period, financial support was generously provided by the National Institute of Mental Health (Grants M1090 and MH08061). Additional aid from the Wisconsin Alumni Research Foundation, the National Science Foundation, and the John Simon Guggenheim Foundation made it possible to spend a research leave in Germany during 1957.

The preparation of the manuscript was significantly facilitated by the willing efforts of my wife Eileen, whose skill in producing readable and grammatically correct copy from unbelievably rough drafts was invaluable. Miss Sharon Toffey and Miss Kathleen Meneghini, graduate students at the Pennsylvania State University, read the manuscript at various stages and made many helpful suggestions for improving its style and content.

Mr. Joseph E. Britt, Jr., The Macmillan Company editor, and Professor Melvin H. Marx, editor of the series, were not only encouraging and similarly helpful, but extremely patient as well.

Finally the author is especially grateful to Professor Clarence H. Graham, who, during the writer's graduate training at Columbia University, introduced him to this field and provided guidance, at a critical time, in the principles of the scientific analysis of behavior.

HERSCHEL W. LEIBOWITZ

Contents

PART ONE: Inquiry and Argument

I. ADAPTATION TO THE PERCEPTUAL WORLD   3
II. INNATE ASPECTS OF PERCEPTION   10
III. THE LEARNING PROCESS IN PERCEPTION   18
IV. PERCEPTUAL SELECTIVITY   28
V. MOTIVATION AND ITS ROLE IN PERCEPTION   35
VI. ILLUSIONS: THE FALLIBILITY OF PERCEPTION   42
VII. PERCEPTION IN MODERN TECHNOLOGY   50
VIII. PERCEPTION AND THE NERVOUS SYSTEM   56

PART TWO: The Selected Readings

[1] "The Perception of Objects," E. G. Boring   67
[2] "Apparent Visual Size as a Function of Distance for Children and Adults," H. P. Zeigler and H. W. Leibowitz   86
[3] "Adaptation to Disarranged Eye-Hand Coordination in the Distance-Dimension," R. Held and M. Schlank   91

xii *Contents*

[4] "The Effects of Attitudes on Descriptions of Pictures,"
     C. Leuba and *C. Lucas*   96
[5] "The Honi Phenomenon: A Case of Selective Perceptual
     Distortion," *W. J. Wittreich*   105
[6] "The Moon Illusion, II," *I. Rock* and *L. Kaufman*   120
[7] "Machines Cannot Fight Alone," *S. S. Stevens*   144
[8] "Relations Between the Central Nervous System and the
     Peripheral Organs," *E. von Holst*   160

BIBLIOGRAPHY   171

INDEX   175

VISUAL PERCEPTION

PART ONE

Inquiry and Argument

CHAPTER I

Adaptation to the Perceptual World

THE ASSIGNMENT OF A "PURPOSE" TO A BIOLOGICAL process is always a risky procedure, and a thorough discussion of the purpose of perception would be beyond the scope of this book. However, in a less rigorous sense, it does not seem unreasonable to assume that one of the goals and purposes of perception is to stabilize our awareness of the world about us in the interest of successful adjustment. In any event, this assumption seems to be a valuable working hypothesis. It is in this context that we observe one of the most interesting aspects of perception. As we move about in the world, there is focused on the inside of our eyes, or, more correctly, on the mass of sense cells known as the retina, optical images of the objects at which we are looking. These images are formed according to known laws of optics. When an object moves away from us, the image becomes smaller. Similarly, as the illumination is varied, the intensity of light in the retinal image changes accordingly. As an object is tilted, its physical image is progressively flattened. These optical relationships, which are predictable from elementary physics, can also be observed if one takes the excised eye of an animal and points it at various objects while observing the image formed on the retina (Boring, 1942). (One must use a fresh eye because of the inevitable clouding of the lens after removal of the blood supply.) In other words, the optical system of the eye is analagous in many respects to a camera or any other optical system that focuses an image (Wald, 1950).

However, in everyday life, we simply do not observe the changes that take place due to these physical transformations. People appear to be about the same size as the distance from us changes despite the predictable variation in the size of the retinal image. As the distance between the eye and an object is varied, the size of the corresponding retinal image varies proportionately. When a person is moving about a normal-sized room, his distance from us frequently varies between two and twenty feet. Under these conditions, the size of the corresponding retinal image changes tenfold. However, we do not perceive a size change of this magnitude—in most cases, the individual appears to remain the same size. Thus, despite the variation in the size of the retinal image, perceived size tends to remain invariant. This phenomenon is referred to in the literature as size constancy, meaning simply that perceived size tends to remain constant at varying observation distances.

In Part Two E. G. Boring [1] [1] describes the history and the biological significance of the phenomenon of size constancy, as well as the implications of the constancies for perceptual theory. In reading this article, it will help to bear in mind that it was written by psychology's historian specifically for an audience of physicists. Boring emphasizes the critical point that perception does not depend solely on the physical characteristics of stimulation, but on other factors as well.

The biological significance of size constancy is clearly that of stabilizing the visual world by emphasizing in our awareness the permanent qualities of objects rather than their continually changing retinal image characteristics. Size constancy can readily be demonstrated with the aid of two coins of the same denomination. Place one coin on the table surface at approximately arm's length and the second, on the other side of the table, as far away as possible. With your hand halfway between your eye and the nearer coin, line up the tips of thumb and index finger so that you enclose the edges of the nearer coin. Without changing the distance of your

[1] Bracketed numbers refer to readings in Part Two.

hand from your eye, shift your gaze to the more distant coin. It will be observed that the "size" of the coins, as measured by the distance between your fingertips, is quite different. Despite this difference, which is roughly proportional to retinal image size, the coins appear to be the same size at different distances. Any two similar-sized objects, indoors or outdoors, can be used for this demonstration.

Size constancy has been investigated for many years, and is known to be manifested by adults, under normal viewing conditions, up to a distance of 50 to 100 feet or more. One might ask by what process size constancy is mediated in the human organism. On this point, there is less agreement in the literature. Nevertheless, we can specify one necessary condition for the appearance of size constancy—it is essential to view not only the object itself but the context surrounding the object. This can be demonstrated, for example, with the two coins described above, by viewing them through a small opening that restricts the visual field to the stimulus itself by cutting off surrounding areas. Such a device, called a reduction screen in psychological literature, can be made by simply punching a hole in a piece of paper with a sharp pencil. Observing through such a reduction screen reduces size constancy in the direction one would predict from the laws of optics. That is, objects farther away appear smaller when viewed through a reduction screen than they would under ordinary viewing conditions.

The implication of these experiments is that the surrounding context, even though one may not be aware of it, is nevertheless critical in maintaining the size constancy effect. (See also the figure on page 139.) This is remarkable, because we do not usually consider the fact that objects to which we do not attend have such important effects on perception. As is true of many phenomena in psychology, experiments demonstrate facts that we would not normally assume from "common sense" to be true.

Another important factor in size constancy is the role of experience. In his classical book on vision, the great German scientist, Hermann von Helmholtz (1962a), describes a phenomenon that occurred when he was being taken to church as a child. He mistook people standing in the belfry for dolls and asked his mother to reach up and get them for him. It would appear from Helmholtz's personal experience that size constancy is not well developed in young children. However, the experimental literature on size constancy has not always supported the implications of Helmholtz's childhood observations. Some of the earlier studies suggested that size constancy for children is as well developed as it is for adults, but these studies were not made at longer observation distances comparable to those at which the young Helmholtz observed his statue. On the assumption that differences in the distance of observation could be responsible for this discrepancy, Zeigler and Leibowitz [2] conducted a study, using a wide range of observation distances, up to 100 feet. The data, which are plotted on page 89, confirm both Helmholtz and the earlier experimental studies. For near-observation distances, size constancy for eight-year-old children is indistinguishable from that for adults. However, as observation distance is increased, the childrens' data show progressively less constancy, while the data for the adults are essentially unaffected. Size constancy develops first for near and then, with experience, for progressively more distant objects. The results of this and similar studies imply that in some way experience with or in the environment is a necessary condition for the development of the size constancy phenomenon.

Although it would be misleading to give the impression that we completely understand how size constancy is mediated, it is reasonable to assume that at least two factors are relevant: the presence of contextual stimuli simultaneously present in the visual field and experience observing such stimuli. Apparently, in some way, we "learn" to take into account the entire context as a basis for the size-constancy effect. More generally, these studies imply that the perceptual process is by no means a passive one. If one were to attempt to predict perception from a simple knowledge of optics, the results would be grossly inaccurate. Although the eye is analogous to a camera to the extent that it focuses an image on the retina, the effects shown here of context and experience illustrate very well the important principle that *the organism itself contributes significantly to the process of perception.*

Constancy of size is only one example of this important biological phenomenon. As we move about our environment, there are gross changes in the amount of light falling on the objects that we view. Even during the daylight hours, when we move from the sunlight outdoors to a room illuminated by artificial light, there may be a change in the intensity of illumination by a factor of a 1,000 to 1. If we consider the difference between bright sunlight and the amount of light available on a moonless night, the difference may increase to as much as 1 billion to one. As in the case of size constancy, we simply do not perceive these great differences in illumination. Consider, for example, a man wearing a white shirt standing in the sunlight holding a piece of coal. If we were to measure the amount of light reflected from his shirt and from the coal, we would see that the quantity is approximately 100 times higher for the shirt than for the coal. Now if the same man goes into a dimly illuminated cellar, which would produce perhaps 1/1,000 of the light available in the sunlight, and again takes readings from the shirt and the coal, proportionately the same figures would be obtained. We know from experience that coal looks black, or dark, and a white shirt looks white, or light, under any condition. However, a physical measurement of the reflected light would indicate that there is actually more light coming from the coal in the sunlight than from the shirt in the basement. Thus, our perception is *not* predictable from the physics of the situation and does not follow from the amount of luminous energy reflected from these objects. Instead, there is a tendency in perception to preserve the constant appearance of brightness or whiteness of objects—an analogy to the phenomenon of size constancy in maintaining the stability of visual perception. Again, the understanding of this effect is not complete, but we do know that as in the case of size perception, context is extremely important. If one performs the reduction screen experiment, brightness constancy is lost. The shirt in the cellar would look dark, and the coal in the sunlight would appear light.

A related phenomenon is that of color constancy. Although we are not usually aware of it, the "color" of illumination varies significantly during the day, being redder at daybreak and at twilight and bluer during midday. Even more strikingly, indoor illumination may be quite different in color from the illumination produced by the sun, being generally redder than sunlight. Ordinarily, we do not observe these differences. However, if one wishes to take realistic color photographs, careful attention to the color of the illumination is necessary in order to avoid distortions. One must use different types of color film for indoor than for outdoor illumination, even for amateur photographs. If the appropriate film is not used, for example, if "indoor" film is employed to take a photograph outdoors, the resulting colors will have an unnatural bluish cast. Likewise, if outdoor film is used indoors, the photographs will appear unnaturally red. Descriptively, we might say that the different films are required because our color constancy is not as good when viewing photographs of a scene than when viewing the scene itself. (For a detailed treatment, see Evans, 1948.) This statement, however, does not explain how color constancy is mediated. Psychologists think that context, as in the case of brightness and size constancy, is important as well as our "memory" for the color of an object. The absence of "memory color" for new clothing once generated many complaints in the retail clothing industry. Clothing first viewed under indoor illumination seemed to be a different shade of color when viewed in daylight. After some experience with the clothing, memory color becomes effective, and the apparent changes in color under different illuminations become less apparent. In recent years, this problem has been minimized by improved artificial illumination, which more nearly approximates the color of outdoor light.

Another important manifestation of the tendency to stabilize perception is the constancy of shape. If a square object is tilted at successively more acute angles, the retinal image will be distorted. The fact is that we do not notice these distortions nor are we aware that round shapes such as the top of a glass will be imaged as ellipses or flattened circles on the retina when viewed at an angle. The tendency to perceive the constant shapes of objects, despite distortion of the retinal image as the angle of observation changes, is called shape constancy (Thouless, 1931, Graham, 1951).

The explanation, or more likely, the explanations for the various aspects of constancy that we have discussed, such as size, brightness, color, and shape, have only been partially identified to date. We do know that although the mechanisms may turn out to be quite different for the various aspects of constancy, one fact is clear —they all serve to stabilize the perception of the visual world. The constancies permit us to react to the stable physical characteristics of objects, an ability of great importance in adjusting to our environment. If we were to perceive the continually changing retinal image characteristics of our environment, which would occur in the absence of constancy, the result would be chaos.

The perceptual constancies manifest themselves, as one might expect, among animals as well as humans. Fish have been shown to demonstrate color constancy; chickens, brightness constancy; and monkeys, shape constancy (Katz, 1937, Osgood, 1953, Zeigler & Leibowitz, 1958). To the knowledge of the writer, no animal has ever failed to demonstrate constancy experimentally. Indeed, it would be difficult to imagine the successful adjustment of any form of animal life that did not have the ability to react to the stable, fixed characteristics of its environment.

The study of perceptual constancy is important for a number of reasons. It serves as an excellent example of the active nature of perception, a reoccurring theme in this essay; it also illustrates that the optics and physics of stimulation tell us very little about perception in the intact organism; it demonstrates the important fact that one need not be aware of the mechanisms underlying perception. Most individuals first hear about perceptual constancy in psychology classes. The many who never hear of it are not in any way inconvenienced in their everyday lives by the lack of this information. Fortunately, the biological value of constancy does not demand knowledge of its presence. Finally, perceptual constancy is of critical importance to our understanding of living organisms, because its presence differentiates mechanical from biological systems. When we know more about the mechanisms of constancy, we will have made significant progress toward understanding the enigma of biology. Perhaps we could even build better mechanical devices if we understood how this important biological process is mediated in living systems. To be sure, the study of the perceptual constancies is interesting and important, as well as challenging.

II

Innate Aspects of Perception

ONE OF THE MOST VIGOROUS AND, AT TIMES, BITTER controversies in the history of psychology has been the question of whether behavior is innate, that is, unlearned, or whether it can be learned or acquired from experience. We know now that the problem is not so simple, that such a dichotomy oversimplifies it. There are many examples of behavior that are strongly influenced by innate tendencies. In particular, lower forms of animal life exhibit many complex behavior patterns usually referred to as instincts. As we ascend the phylogenetic scale, we find fewer examples of the complex, unlearned behavior patterns that are so prevalent in lower forms. However, innate factors are present at all levels, and the question remains as to the relative contribution of innate and learned characteristics in the development of behavior for all species.

In the field of perception, there are many examples of innate perceptual responses in lower forms. One of the most striking examples is to be found in the behavior of the honey bee. In the normal activity of the beehive, "scout bees" go out to search for sources of food. When they find food—for example, a field of flowers in bloom —they return to the hive and communicate the direction and distance of the food source to other bees by means of a dance. Figure 1 illustrates the communication dances of the bees (von Frisch, 1950). As the scout bee moves through this pattern, other bees follow, touching their antennae to the scout and picking up information as to the direction and distance of the food source. The "coding" of direction and distance information is fascinating. With respect to direction, the position of the straight portion of the dance is significant. The rule is that the straight portion of the dance is oriented at the same angle of gravity (the dance is performed on a vertical comb of the hive) as the angle the bee has flown with respect to the sun. The exact relationship here is less important than

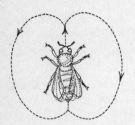 

FIGURE 1. *Left:* The tail-wagging communication dance of the honey bee. The number of turns is an indicator of distance; the fewer turns, the farther away the food source. *Right:* The round dance indicating that food is nearby. (Reprinted from *Bees—Their Vision, Chemical Senses, and Language* by Karl von Frisch. Copyright 1950 by Cornell University. Used by permission of Cornell University Press.)

the variables involved. The bees can innately perceive the position of the sun when outdoors and orient their dance so as to communicate, in the dark, to other bees the relationship between the angle of the sun and the angle of flight. The recipients of this message then emerge from the hive and fly in the appropriate direction. Distance is coded in two ways. If the food is nearby, the bees perform a different dance pattern, the round dance. A second and more precise indicator of distance is the number of turns made during the dance. The more turns, the closer the food.

Such complex behavior is astounding even to an experienced student of instinctive behavior in insects. Professor Karl von Frisch, who has devoted the major portion of a distinguished career to the study of the bee, was so amazed at his discovery of this means of communication that he remarked that no competent scientist should believe this study the first time he hears it! Although von Frisch, whose research techniques are a model of scientific excellence, probably questioned his findings at first, his subsequent work has removed all doubts. Bees do, in fact, transmit information regarding the direction and distance of food by means of dances. To many scientists, this discovery by von Frisch is of unrivaled importance in biology. In further studies, von Frisch discovered that different species of bees have slightly different methods of communication; although they all communicate by dancing, the details of the pattern depend on the species. Language dialects exist even in the world of insects! (von Frisch, 1962).

Innate perceptual responses also exist in higher forms of life. Fish exhibit many varied and interesting instincts. For example, the zoologist Niko Tinbergen, of Oxford University, has studied the fighting behavior of the male stickleback fish. He points out that the characteristic fighting behavior of the male stickleback is directed primarily against other males and not against females. The question is how the animal makes this discrimination. Tinbergen conjectured that the basis for the discrimination is the fact that males of the species have a red throat and belly. This hypothesis was tested by constructing models of sticklebacks some of which were very poor imitations, lacking many of the characteristics of the species, even of fish in general. Nevertheless, the male stickleback would attack a model with a red belly that, to us, did not even resemble a fish more often than it would attack an accurate imitation of the stickleback that lacked the red color. In effect, this experiment puts into competition the red color against other morphological characteristics of the animal. The results show that the fish react innately to the red while neglecting the other characteristics (Tinbergen, 1951).

Students of animal behavior refer to the ability of certain stimuli to energize instinctive patterns of behavior as "releasers." Releasers are defined as stimuli of various shapes and colors that serve the specific function, as illustrated in the fighting behavior of the stickleback, of triggering an appropriate sequence of behavior in another member of the same species. Learning is thought to play no role in their establishment. The display and subsequent reaction to it does not depend on prior experience. Such perceptual releasers play a significant part in activating instincts, especially those concerned with mating and maternal behavior. A number of releasers have been identified and studied. According to Tinbergen, the gaping reaction of young thrushes, a response that permits the mother to drop food into the young bird's mouth, is released by an object greater than 3 mm in diameter, moving above the bird's eyes. The sexual pursuit of the male grayling butterfly is released by a dark, fluttering object, the color, size, or shape of which is not important. The releasing stimulus is highly specific and most often represents only a small part of the total stimulus complex (Tinbergen, 1951).

Instinctive perceptual behavior is also shown by birds. Among the best known examples of instincts in birds is their ability to migrate over great distances at the appropriate time of the year. In recent years, a number of facts regarding the basis for migration has been uncovered (Griffin, 1948). One of the puzzling aspects of this problem, however, is the identification of the cues used by the animals to find their way. We know that human beings must rely on relatively complex navigational aids when traveling by air. How, then, do birds accomplish this same feat? It has been shown that the sun is an important cue used by birds, and even fish, for navigational purposes. Apparently, the animals have an "inner clock" that allows them to "calculate" their orientation from the position of the sun and awareness of the time of day. (See the volume *Biological Clocks*, 1960.)

The use of the sun as a navigational cue is most interesting. One wonders what sort of nervous mechanism common to bees, fish, and birds permits not only an awareness of time but supports the complex processes required to compare the position of the sun with the time of day and to "calculate" the desired direction of migration. As if this situation were not already sufficiently complex, some birds —for example, the warbler—migrate at night and cannot make use of the sun. A logical possiblity would be that these birds utilize the stars for navigation. Dr. Franz Sauer tested this hypothesis by observing the warblers in a planetarium, a dome-shaped building inside of which it was possible to project realistic star patterns of the heavens (Sauer, 1958, Sauer & Sauer, 1960). The warbler, when placed in the planetarium, would position its body in the direction appropriate for migration, north in the spring, and south in the fall.

Apparently the bird is able *innately* to perceive and interpret the position of the stars in the sky and to use this information to indicate the direction of north and south. That this ability is truly innate is demonstrated by the fact that the birds can make the appropriate response independent of experience. A most adaptive and amazing ability!

Although the innate perceptual capacities of lower animals may seem incredible to the human being, one must bear in mind that such animals do not have the "luxury" of long periods of learning. For animals in which instincts are common, the maturation period between birth and adulthood is relatively short. The instinctive perceptual behavior permits the animal to adjust to its environment by means of built-in responses rather than by relying on more time-consuming learned behavior. It also helps to keep in mind, in reflecting on these incredibly adaptive innate responses, that the sun and the stars are probably the most consistent perceptual stimuli present in the history of the world. During the millions of years of evolution, the species might well be expected to have adapted to the most reliable indication of direction available. This, of course, does not explain how inner clocks and sun compasses operate in the tiny brain of the bird or the rudimentary nervous system of the bee, but the evolutionary approach does provide a framework within which these behaviors can be conceptualized and related to other facts of biology.

When we move to higher forms of life, the question of innate behavior is complicated by the fact that such species exhibit an increasing tendency to profit from experience. It has been stated that even if human beings do, in fact, have instincts, these tendencies are so modified by learning and experience that they cannot be compared with the fixed behavioral patterns prevalent in lower forms. Nevertheless, when one looks carefuly at mammals, and even humans, examples of innate perceptual abilities can be demonstrated.

Drs. Eleanor J. Gibson and Richard Walk at Cornell University have recently proven that the perception of depth is innate in young mammals (Gibson & Walk, 1960). This was accomplished by constructing an apparatus in which a solid center support is surrounded on both sides by "cliffs." Although the animal is protected from danger by a sturdy glass cover if it should leave the center support, it can see down into the cliff. The cliffs on either side of the support are of different depths, one shallow and the other deep. The child or animal looking over the side of the cliffs sees the same perceptual pattern in both cases, with the exception that one is farther away than the other. The question to be answered is whether the subject will leave the safety of the center support and venture over the apparent void of the cliff. If it does, which side will it prefer, the shallow or deep? If the shallow side is preferred, it would suggest that the perception of depth is innate in this subject. A number of species have been tested, including chickens, rats, cats, goats, and human infants. In all cases, there is a tendency to avoid the deep cliff and to prefer the shallow one, suggesting that the perception of depth is not only innate, but that its dangerous implications are meaningful to the young animal. It is not recommended on the basis of this study that the young child be permitted to play in high places in the belief that he will be protected by his instinctive avoidance of cliffs. These experiments were carefully designed to equalize all cues except for those of distance—the real-life situation presents many additional variables. However, the results do demonstrate that even higher forms of life can exhibit innate perceptual tendencies.

A final question to be considered is the way in which innate and learned capacities contribute to perceptual development. For example, we know that the accurate perception of the human face is a most important attribute in the human being. Robert Fantz, a psychologist at Western Reserve University, recently made significant contributions to our understanding of this area (Fantz, 1961, 1965). Fantz has developed an elegantly simple method of studying the perceptual development of infants. By observing the position of the eyes, he can determine in which direction they are looking. Assuming that the direction of gaze indicates some awareness on the part of the child, he has presented young infants with choices of patterns to view. For example, a white or colored circle versus an outline drawing of a human face, newsprint versus a circle. Interestingly enough, infants, even those under five days of age, prefer to look at facelike objects. These results have important implications for our theories about the development of perception. They indicate that, first of all, the child *can see something*. If infant vision were, indeed, a "booming, buzzing confusion," as was previously thought to be the case, there should be no preference of any kind exhibited—all would be a meaningless blur. Evidently, some pattern vision is available at least within five days of birth. Secondly, there appear to be innate preferences for certain types of patterns, in particular for those which resemble a human face. This tendency is of obvious biological value to the developing infant, because much of our information about other people comes from the face. We identify individuals, determine whether they are paying attention to us, ascertain their agreement or disagreement with us, and obtain indications of their feelings and thoughts by looking for cues from their faces. An innate tendency to single out the face, among all the stimuli available to the child, would be of value in directing his attention and shaping his awareness of this most important perceptual stimulus.

To the student of general psychology, a consideration of innate perceptual behavior should present few new concepts. Just as is the case for behavior in general, innate perceptual tendencies complement and balance the ability of any species to profit from experience. The lower forms that have a relatively short maturation period are dominated by instincts and have comparatively little ability to profit from experience. As we ascend the phylogenetic scale, learning becomes increasingly important, and instinctive behavior is progressively less conspicuous. Although all animals learn, from the amoeba to the human, and all animals exhibit innate tendencies, the relative emphasis on nature and nurture shifts predictably along the phylogenetic scale. For the reader who, at this point, may agree with von Frisch's advice that no competent scientist should believe at first glance the stories about the behavior of the bee or, for that matter, of the innate perceptual tendencies of the fish or the bird, there is a redeeming feature to this story. Although any one instinct, or any one example of behavior, may seem incredible when considered by itself, the overall picture shows some semblance of order and regularity. Living organisms *do* adapt to their environments. The relative importance of the mechanisms of adaptation is adjusted appropriately to the duration of the life cycle of the species. If the bee had to learn navigation, it would cease to exist. If human behavior were locked in by instinctive patterns, our modern civilization, with its infinite variety of cultures and customs, would be impossible, and our entire concept of man as we understand him would be meaningless. Consideration of the role of innate tendencies in perception fits nicely into the biological concept of behavior, a welcome concurrence in a field with so many unsolved problems.

CHAPTER III

The Learning Process in Perception

IF ONE TAKES A BROAD OVERALL VIEW OF CONTEMPO-
rary psychology, it is striking to observe how much of the activity in
this field is concerned with the phenomenon of learning. The human
being is particularly able to profit from experience, and learning
plays a major role in the life of our species. The importance of
learning applies equally well to perception—we have already seen
how, in children, the tendency toward size constancy can be learned.
Although animals have many innate perceptual tendencies, they are
also capable of modifying their behavior as a result of experience.

Examples of learning among animals are numerous and, at
times, startling. The Swiss physician and naturalist August Forel
noticed more than 50 years ago that bees would appear on the
veranda of his house at breakfast time looking for food. They appeared at the same time each day, as if they had learned and could
remember what time food would be available to them. On the basis
of this observation, it has been suggested that bees posses a "time
sense" or an "inner clock" that allows them to tell the time of day and
to adjust their activities accordingly. This time sense of bees was
tested by the German zoologist Max Renner (1960) in an experiment in which he constructed two identical rooms, one of which
was set up in Paris, France, and the other, in New York City. He

then fed bees daily in the Paris room between 8:15 P.M. and 10:15 P.M. As would be expected from Forel's observations, the bees soon learned to emerge from their hive promptly at 8:15 P.M. to gather food and then to return to their hive at 10:15 P.M., when the food was no longer available. Renner was then ready for a critical test of the time sense. If bees really possessed an inner clock, they should continue to look for food between 8:15 P.M. and 10:15 P.M., Paris time, despite changes in their environment. Within the same day, thanks to modern jet transportation, Renner was able to transport his bees to New York and to place them in a room identical to that in which they had been trained in Paris. The crucial question was, when would the bees emerge? Would they look for food according to Paris time, or would the rapid 3,000-mile trip in jet plane and taxi distort their time perception? Renner reported that the bees were not at all confused. At 8:15 P.M., Paris time, "they came out of their hive and flew around the room as if they had never been moved." The perception of time in this species is remarkable. It does not depend on cues from the sun, temperature, gravity, or any other known external factors, because all of these were well controlled by Renner. It depends, apparently, on an ability to perceive accurately the passage of time. This ability is obviously of great importance to the animal, because it permits it to regulate its food-seeking activities according to the time of day that food is available.

Another challenging problem for the student of animal behavior is the explanation of the ability of fish to migrate. The American zoologist Arthur Hasler states the problem as follows: "The Chinook salmon of the U.S. Northwest is born in a small stream, migrates downriver to the Pacific Ocean as a young smolt, and, after as long as five years, swims back unerringly to the stream of its birth to spawn. . . . How do they find their way back, sometimes from 800 to 900 miles away?" (Hasler & Larsen, 1955). On the basis of research by Hasler and Warren Wisby (1951), we suspect that this ability depends on the sense of smell, which is extremely acute in fish. Salmon with their noses plugged with cotton fail to return to the stream of their birth. Further evidence that odor is the critical factor comes from laboratory studies. It is possible to train fish to distinguish water taken from various streams. Although the chemical constituents of the various waters cannot be identified, differences do exist that can be perceived by the salmon. A fish migrating up-stream could, conceivably, be guided by the memory of the odor of the water in which it was spawned and attained maturity. At least the perceptual basis for this ability exists, and it does appear to be a likely explanation for this old problem.

As is frequently the case in the development of science, important discoveries are often made by chance. In the early part of this century, considerable public attention was attracted to an unusual horse named Clever Hans, that, it was reputed, could perform arithmetical calculations, tell time, and even analyze music (Katz, 1937). The horse's owner had worked out a special system of com-munication because, despite his reputed intelligence, Hans had not learned to speak. The owner would ask the horse, for example, what was the day of the month. The horse would then tap his foot until the number of taps equaled the date. The owner was convinced that horses were as intelligent as men and needed only the proper education to take advantage of their abilities. A commission of eminent zoologists and psychologists examined the horse and re-ported that the performance of the animal was legitimate. In fact, the horse would answer questions posed by anyone; it was not even necessary for the owner to ask the question. Before the reader pe-titions his local school board to admit horses to classrooms, it should be pointed out that a necessary condition for the horse's perform-ance was seeing his owner while tapping out the answers. If the owner stepped behind a screen so as to block the horse's view, the horse simply tapped indefinitely. What happened was that the owner, in anticipation of the correct response, inadvertently made slight movements of his head that were perceived by the horse as a signal to stop tapping. This was the kind of anticipatory move-ment similar to the reaction of a parent watching a child repeat a poem or song from memory. These movements were made quite by accident and were very small. However, the horse, although not as clever as the owner had assumed, did have the perceptual ca-pacity to look for and respond to the unwitting cues provided by the owner. The Clever Hans story is valuable not only as an ex-ample of perceptual learning, but as a reminder that the perceptual abilities of animals must be considered before assuming that their remarkable achievements are the result of higher intellect.

Examples of perceptual learning in animals are numerous. The owners of dogs and cats are only too eager to relate stories praising the abilities of their pets. Many of these stories, even if one allows for the biased effect of the master's motivation on his perception of the pet's behavior, are nevertheless remarkable and pose interesting questions for the student of perception. How can a dog or cat find its way home after roaming the streets of a city for hours or even days? How do birds, released many miles from their nests, find their way back swiftly and accurately? The final answer to these questions will depend on a more complete knowledge of the perceptual learning capacities of these species than is now available. Although rich in anecdotes, the perceptual behavior of animals is, at the same time, a fertile field for further scientific analysis.

Among humans, many dramatic forms of learning can be demonstrated. An excellent example is based on the fact that the image on the retina is inverted. This is true because the eye, having a positive lens system, produces a real but inverted image. This phenomenon, since its discovery by the famous French philosopher Descartes in the seventeenth century, has interested and puzzled students of perception. In the latter part of the last century, experiments were performed in which special glasses were worn so that the retinal image was erect rather than inverted. This is accomplished by inverting the image before it reaches the eye so that when the eye goes through its normal process of inversion, the end product is an erect retinal image. More recently, the Austrian psychologist, Ivo Kohler, has repeated and extended some of these early experiments. He has shown, in confirmation of earlier studies, that after a relatively short period of confusion, including some discomfort and even sickness, the subject learns to adjust to the inverted image so that he is able to move about normally even though the world appears upside down. More strikingly, after an even longer period of time, the world actually appears right side up. This entire process, given the appropriate conditions for relearning, can take place in less than one week. When the inverting glasses are removed, the world again appears upside down, but relearning is accomplished quickly.

The inverted image experiments demonstrate several important principles. First of all, in relation to much of the earlier discussions about this phenomenon, it proves that in the nervous system there is no fixed up or down with regard to the perception of the retinal image. The old philosophical problem of how we can see right side up when the image is upside down has meaning only if one assumes that the brain responds uniquely to the direction of the retinal image. The inversion experiments suggest that visual direction is learned and that the orientation of the retinal image is not critical to our perception of upness or downness.

Secondly, the studies show us the extent to which we can relearn visual habits. The subjects in the inversion experiments were adults who had many years of visual experience with an inverted retinal image. In the course of less than a week, they were able essentially to relearn habits that had been practiced during their entire lifetimes and to adjust successfully to a completely new mode of retinal image orientation. This emphasizes the extremely important contribution of the learning process to perception and suggests, furthermore, that learning normally plays an important part in perceptual development. The assumption is simply that if a process can be retained or changed, it is reasonable to assume that we are dealing with a learned phenomenon.

The experiments of Kohler and others in this field have also indicated some of the conditions under which perceptual learning and relearning take place. For example, in the Kohler experiment, a subject who had been wearing the glasses for a day or so would see the world as upside down if he sat passively looking about. However, as soon as he moved and touched the objects around him, the world seemed to "flip over" and appear erect. It would seem, therefore, that a necessary condition for relearning is active movement of the individual. A passive observer wearing inverting glasses would be expected to relearn and adjust extremely slowly, if at all. This line of reasoning has been recently extended in a most interesting series of experiments by Professor Richard Held and his colleagues [3].[1] Held substituted for the inverting lens prisms that displace the apparent position of objects in the visual field. A subject wearing such prisms will at first miss the mark when he reaches for objects. After a period of time, as in the inversion experiments,

[1] Bracketed numbers refer to readings in Part Two.

the subject adjusts to the glasses and performs normally. The contribution of Held has been to specify the conditions under which relearning actually takes place. He devised a simple testing box illustrated on page 93. The subject looking into this box observes a mirror in which is reflected an image of a target. If a subject attempts to indicate by marking with a pencil where the target is, he will do so with a negligibly small error. If, however, he wears prisms that displace the image to the right, he will make a predictable error in locating the target away from its true position.

Using this apparatus, Held discovered that one of the important conditions for adjusting to the displacement of the prism is the self-activated movement of the subject. For example, if the subject wears the prisms and moves about normally, he will soon adjust to the displacement of the prisms and gradually locate the target in its true position. If, however, the subject sits passively, or is moved about by someone else, for example in a wheelchair, very little, if any, relearning takes place. Held emphasizes that relearning is dependent upon the self-initiated activity of the individual. By inference, the visual-motor learning of the child is also aided by his self-produced movement. Perhaps the typically energetic activity of young children is necessary for normal visual-motor learning!

The extent to which perception is learned, although strikingly demonstrated in these experiments, is not adequately conveyed by laboratory studies. Consider, for example, the fact that human beings can easily recognize individuals by their faces. In fact, the human face is the most frequently used perceptual stimulus on identification cards, in school yearbooks, and even in the familiar "wanted" posters that appear in federal post offices. On what basis do we make such discriminations? This is a question of considerable practical importance, not only for purposes of identification, but from a theoretical point of view. Unfortunately, there are no experiments in perception that will now permit us to analyze fruitfully this situation. We do know, however, that this phenomenon is learned, that it can be acquired by young children, and that once learned it can be extremely stable. Consider that it is possible to recognize individuals one has not seen for 20 or 30 years despite the passing of time and the inevitable changes in appearance. It is certain that future research in perception will be directed toward this problem. At present, we must be content simply to point out that this is a dramatic example of percepual learning.

Although we are not able to explain how the recognition of the human face takes place, we do have some information regarding the analagous phenomenon in the field of auditory perception. If you hear someone with whose voice you are familiar greet you with the word *hello,* chances are that you can identify the speaker quickly and accurately without seeing him. For individuals whom we know, only a few words are required to establish their identity. This ability is not confined to human beings. It is a relatively simple matter to train a dog to respond only to the commands given by one individual. Evidently there are sufficient differences in the voices of individuals to allow for accurate discrimination.

Progress toward identification of the physical basis of this phenomenon has recently been reported by Dr. L. G. Kersta of the Bell Telephone Laboratories (Kersta, 1962). Dr. Kersta has discovered that the physical attributes of speech are almost as characteristic of the individual as his fingerprints. Dr. Kersta makes "voice prints" that reveal the pattern of voice energy at the various levels of pitch. Such prints, made by various individuals, are so unique that they can be matched visually as a means of positive identification of the speaker. It is not possible to alter one's voice print by disguising the voice. Although it is possible to mimic another individual so that the voices *sound* the same, the voice prints remain typical of the speaker. Although this field is relatively new, it is not unreasonable to assume that future research will permit as accurate identification with voice prints as is now possible with fingerprints.

The ability to identify the minute variations in the voice of another individual is not confined to the human species. Paul Mundinger of Cornell University has recently discovered that this ability also exists in the American goldfinch. A member of this species is able to differentiate the calls of its mate from those of other members of the species. According to Mundinger, the goldfinch forms pair bonds approximately two months before nesting takes place. "Throughout this long 'engagement' period, and during nest building and incubation, the pair can maintain vocal contact. The male when in flight utters a flight call, and when the female is perched or incubating, she will respond to the male's flight call with a characteristic vocalization."

In order to test whether the female will respond only to her own male's vocalization, Mundinger played back to ovulating or incubating females the taped recordings of their mates, as well as recordings made by other males, and observed the response by the female. The data suggest that the female can single out and respond to the recorded call of her own mate as different from that of other males. Although, as is the case with humans, we do not ordinarily identify individuals on the basis of vocal cues alone, sufficient subtle differences in voice quality can apparently form the basis for accurate identification.

Mundinger states further: "In the field, I can recognize individual males by their characteristic vocal quality and the pattern of their flight call. I have never definitely heard a female respond to a male other than her own mate even though for periods of 20–30 minutes five to eight or more males may fly over her calling the flight call." Although, the identifying physical characteristics that form the basis for this adaptive discrimination have not been analyzed, it is interesting to note the subtle, and perhaps even sentimental, quality of this learned perceptual capacity.

The identification of individuals by means of faces and voices is similar in that both involve perceptual learning. The exact process by which such learning takes place has not been discovered. In fact, only in the case of voice identification can we specify with any reasonable degree of accuracy the stimulus responsible for the discrimination. There are, however, two principles to be learned from these facts. First of all, perceptual learning does take place in the interest of adjustment. It is important for us to recognize individuals, which we can do given the appropriate conditions of experience. Secondly, and perhaps more importantly from the point of view of this essay, we *need not be aware* of the stimuli to which we are responding. Before the work of Kersta, we knew that individuals could be recognized by their voices. Based on Kersta's work, we now have some notion as to the physical basis for the discrimination. However, the observer making a voice identification would never be able to uncover these physical differences—they can only be obtained by elaborate physical analysis such as Kersta's. In general, we learn to respond to and use cues of which we are not aware. Although we use the cues in everyday perception, we cannot identify or describe them verbally, this being a task for experimental analysis.

As indicated in the beginning of this chapter, the phenomenon of learning or modification of behavior by experience is perhaps the most intensively studied problem in modern psychology. Ordinarily, various aspects of learning are treated as separate topics in elementary psychology courses—for example, conditioning, concept formation, verbal learning, perceptual learning, and so on. Although we recognize that the discrete treatment of various areas may be desirable if not necessary from the pedagogical point of view, it should be pointed out that all aspects of learning, no matter how classified, have much in common. For example, the phenomenon of perceptual constancy, a classic topic in perception, may be described as a constant response to a wide variety of physical stimuli. This description bears a definite formal similarity to that of stimulus generalization, in which a variety of stimuli similar to the original conditioning stimulus has the potential of evoking the conditioned response. Similarly, it is highly probable that concepts such as *man, roundness, coal,* and so on, contribute to the phenomena of size, shape, and brightness constancy by associating a number of different stimuli under a given verbal designation. The close relationship to concept formation and verbal learning is obvious (Graham, 1951).

Fortunately, the more we investigate various phenomena in psychology, the more apparent are their similarities. As we learn more about conditioning, stimulus and response generalization, and concept formation, we will be in a better position to appreciate perceptual learning and the perceptual constancies. Conversely, a theory of perceptual constancy that is not consistent with our knowledge of learning in general will be misleading and incomplete. The goal of science is to explain as many phenomena with as few principles as possible. Whether our current theories are adequate, or whether new organizing principles will be needed, can only be determined by future developments. However, it is a good bet that future advances will be characterized by a closer relationship of perceptual learning with the many other categories of modification by experience.

The most important implication of this chapter is that perceptual learning is a field with considerable potential for experimentation. Perception would be of little use to the organism if it were not modifiable by experience. In this respect, it has much in common with other aspects of psychology. This potential represents both a challenge and a hope. We know that human nature is not fixed; that we can better the lot of mankind by the appropriate application of well-established principles of behavioral modification. To accomplish this task, we will need to develop and refine our knowledge of the fundamental facts underlying behavior and experience, a not insignificant aspect of which is the process of perceptual learning.

CHAPTER IV

Perceptual Selectivity

AT ANY ONE MOMENT, OUR SENSE ORGANS ARE RECEIV-
ing various kinds of stimuli. As these lines are being read, there are
probably sounds and odors present; pressures of your chair against
your body; and objects in your environment other than the words
on this page. If you so choose, you can immediately become aware
of them. In other words, you can *select* from among a variety of
stimuli those which you "choose" to permit to enter awareness.
This selective process is not confined to stimulation of the sense
organs. You can also think about events that have taken place in the
past or that will take place in the future. The ability to select from
a wide variety of possible inputs is referred to in the psychological
literature as the process of *attention*. Attention, or selective perception, is an extremely important concept in the study of perception,
because it determines what we are aware of at the moment.

The appropriateness of our attention may at times be rather important, if not critical, to our adjustment. The student in class who
is thinking about something other than the lecture topic may as
well not be in class. The driver whose attention wanders from the
road in front of him may become involved in an accident. A serious
symptom of mental illness occurs when an individual is "compelled"
to pay attention to nonexistent voices or sees objects in the environ-

ment that do not in fact exist. Such false perceptions are called hallucinations. They prevent one from adjusting to his environment, because it is not possible to distinguish hallucinations from true perceptions. Hallucinations may occur as a result of extreme fatigue or as a result of certain drugs or alcohol. However, they usually accompany serious mental illness and should be treated accordingly.

Although psychologists have been aware of the importance of attention for many years, relatively little is known about it. We do know that attention may be influenced by motivation. We perceive to a great extent what we want to perceive. As you travel through the streets of a city, you are more apt to notice the restaurant signs if you are hungry, barber shop or beauty salon signs if your hair needs attention, mail boxes if you want to mail a letter, and so on. In other words, we select from the many possibilities of perception those which relate to our needs at the moment.

Attention is also determined by past experience. A young coed walking on the street of a college town may be perceived as a potential customer by the proprietor of a local dress shop, as a possible date by a male student, or as a future baby sitter by a mother with young children. A hair dresser may notice that the coed's hair is naturally curly; a chiropodist may notice that her feet are flat; and a physician may wonder whether or not a slight skin blemish is an allergic reaction. We do not perceive indiscriminately but rather attend to those factors that have become meaningful to us through past experience. Again we see that the human organism is not a passive receiver of stimuli, a point of view that is also illustrated in other chapters of this essay.

So far in this chapter the discussion has been concerned with examples of the quality of perception, that is, what is perceived. An important aspect of the study of perception has been the determination of how much can be perceived. For example, if you are told that the street number of a house in which you are interested is 135, you will have little difficulty in perceiving and remembering these three digits. Our "span" or "quantity" of attention is greater than three digits. However, if you were told verbally that your student number is 190121573, you would have difficulty in remembering it exactly and would probably ask to have the number repeated so you could make a written record of it. The number of items that can be perceived in a short time period is limited to about seven. If a subject is asked how many dots were flashed on a screen, he could accurately report up to about seven. The subject reports the number immediately with hardly any error (Kaufman, Lord, Reese, & Volkmann, 1949, Miller, 1956). However, if more than seven items are presented, the number of errors increases sharply, and the confidence of the subject in his estimation is reduced. It is interesting to note that some individuals have difficulty in remembering the seven digits usually used for telephone numbers. Since seven is the *average* span of attention, it is not surprising to find individuals for whom seven items exceed their attention capacity.

In everyday life, the selection of items to which we attend is accomplished quickly and without difficulty. We perceive the restaurant or bookstore and act accordingly. It is possible to artificially present an individual with choices that compete for attention and for which no easy selection is possible. An excellent example is the numerous "Mystery Houses" that have been constructed in amusement parks. These place visual cues into conflict with postural and gravitational stimuli. Consider a room of normal rectangular or square construction that has simply been tilted, as in Figure 2. An individual in this unusual room will receive conflicting information regarding which way is up. Gravity would indicate to him that down is as shown by the arrow marked G. On the other hand, because rooms are usually built with vertical walls and we have had extensive past experience with normally vertically oriented walls and horizontally oriented floors and ceilings, we might assume that up and down are indicated by the direction of the walls of the room as illustrated by the arrow marked V. Thus two familiar indices of upness and downness that ordinarily are in harmony are now put into conflict with each other. An observer in such a room is naturally confused. However, perhaps because vision is so critically important for human beings, the conflict is resolved after a few moments in favor of the visual cues. That is, the gravitational cues tend to be ignored, and we assume that the walls, which are actually tilted, are really straight up and down.

At this point, a number of interesting demonstrations is possible, one of which is the "ball that rolls uphill." In Figure 2 the true or

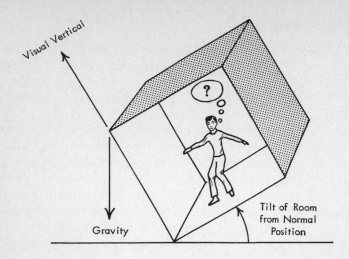

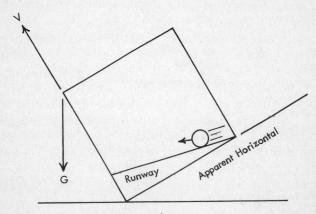

FIGURE 2. *Upper:* A tilted room. The direction of up and down, as given by visual cues, corresponds to the orientation of the walls of the room indicated by *V*. The direction as indicated by gravity is indicated by *G*. *Lower:* Explanation of the "ball that runs uphill." The runway actually slopes to the left in relation to the true horizontal, but *appears* to slope to the right in relation to the apparent horizontal. The ball rolling to the left appears to run uphill!

gravitational vertical or horizontal and the perceived vertical and horizontal are both indicated. Keep in mind that the observer's attention is dominated by the visual cues, and that the gravitational cues tend to be ignored. The runway will then be perceived with

31

reference to the room as slanting *upward,* although in relation to gravity it is really sloping downward, as indicated by its relation to the true horizontal. A ball placed at the right end of the runway will appear to run uphill—a most compelling and dramatic demonstration!

A wide variety of tricks is possible in such a room, many of which can be seen in the commercial amusement houses throughout the United States. For example, water appears to fall at an angle; a pendulum swings through a strange arc; dishes appear to be "pulled" back into a closet, and so on. Observations of these tricks are instructive because they demonstrate what happens when visual and gravitational cues compete for attention and the visual cues predominate. In the amusement parks, the explanations given by the guides who attribute the effects to the existence of large mineral deposits under the earth, faults in the gravitational field, and "mysterious and sinister forces as yet unknown to science" should be considered as show business. A simple but convincing experiment can be performed by closing one's eyes so that the visual cues are eliminated. Immediately the perception of the vertical shifts from the visual direction to the direction determined by gravity. A visit to one of these demonstrations is valuable from both the recreational and scientific points of view.

The relationship between gravitational cues and visual cues is more significant than merely to be considered as the basis for one aspect of an amusement park. In the early days of aviation it was assumed that a pilot flying "blind" at night or in fog could tell which way was up by means of gravitational cues. Unfortunately the movements of the airplane and conflict with the visual cues render the perception of the gravitational upright less accurate, with the results that pilots who thought they were flying normally would emerge from a cloud upside down. Many accidents were thought to be a result of the dependence on gravitational cues. In modern aviation the pilot does not rely on gravitational cues, but rather makes use of vision or, in bad weather, navigational instruments for orientation. It would appear from these observations that when visual cues are in conflict with those of other sensory modalities, the visual cues are more often preferred or attended to. This is probably due to the fact that man is primarily a visual animal—

more information comes to us through our eyes than through any of our other senses.

The study of attention and its disorders is fairly prevalent in modern psychology, although neither the selective aspect of perception nor the process of attention is usually identified as such. For example, studies of distraction in the industrial environment are essentially concerned with attention. A typical question is whether unwanted noise is detrimental to production. In terms of our discussion we might ask to which aspect of stimulation the worker attends, the extraneous noise or the stimulation provided by his work. Essentially the distracting noise presents an alternative possibility for attention, and the choice made by the worker will determine, to a large extent, his productivity (Poffenberger, 1942).

A significant proportion of the effort in advertising industry is directed toward attracting the attention of the consumer. Color, movement, size, and sex and prestige symbols have been shown to have an inherent ability to attract attention and are freely used in advertising media. The manufacturers and merchants are literally competing for the attention of the consumer. It is a basic fact of merchandising that a necessary condition preceding a purchase is an awareness of the product to be offered. An instructive exercise is to analyze advertisements in terms of the bases on which they make their bid for our attention. Roadside billboards or magazine advertisements provide appropriate material for analysis.

Attention also plays a significant role in interpersonal relations. Dale Carnegie, author of the best seller of several decades ago *How To Win Friends and Influence People,* stated that the highest compliment we can pay another individual is to give him our undivided attention. In the present context, we might paraphrase Carnegie and state that it is flattering to an individual when, in competition with all the stimuli that compete for our attention, we choose to listen to him. Either statement is correct and well worth keeping in mind.

Disorders of attention are a common occurrence. Students complain, for example, that they cannot "pay" attention to their professors. It might be asked, then, why the student *selects* to attend to something other than the stimulation provided by the lecturer. Perhaps the student is not interested in or motivated to learn about the subject being discussed. Perhaps the problem has an emotional basis. The lecturer may be dull or the student sleepy. In any event, the *reason* for the inappropriate selection is the goal of the guidance counselor or psychotherapist. Bad habits are also a result of a modification of attention. The chief difficulty with habits such as nail biting is that the individual is simply not aware of what he is doing. The habitual act has been repeated so often that the awareness of it has diminished. A method of treatment is to focus attention on the undesired act by one means or another. The typist who continually types *hte* for *the* is not aware of the error until after it has been committed. In order to correct the mistake it is necessary that she be aware of the act *beforehand.* One method of correction that has been successful is to purposely type the error many times in order to bring the act back into awareness, where it can be consciously avoided (Dunlap, 1932).

The study of attention has exposed the reader to wide variety of phenomena. The ubiquity of the study of perception is well illustrated by the multifarious nature of attention. Whenever we are awake we attend to something. Even in order to read these pages, it was necessary to invoke selective perception. Hopefully this selection will prove to have been worthwhile.

CHAPTER V

Motivation and Its Role
in Perception

THERE IS A FAMILIAR SAYING THAT "WE SEE WHAT WE want to see." Stimulation of the sense organs does not produce, as has been pointed out in this essay, a fixed, mechanical, predictable perceptual experience. Rather, the final awareness resulting from stimulation is subject to various transformations, alterations, and corrections. During this process, the wants, needs, fears, and expectations of the observer have ample opportunity to modify and even distort what is finally perceived. The following incident cited by William James, the pioneer American psychologist, from his own experience, illustrates the effect of uncertainty and perhaps even anxiety on perception: [1]

Sitting, reading, late one night, I suddenly heard a most formidable noise proceeding from the upper part of the house, which it seemed to fill. It ceased, and in a moment renewed itself. I went into the hall to listen, but it came no more. Resuming my seat in the room, however, there it was again, low, light, alarming, like a rising flood, or the *avant-courier* of an awful gale. It came from all space. Quite startled, I again ran into the hall, but it had already ceased once more. On adjourning

[1] William James, *Principles of Psychology* (New York: Holt, Rinehart and Winston, Inc., 1890). Reprinted by Dover Publications, 1950.

to the room the second time, I discovered that it was nothing but the breathing of a little Scotch Terrier which lay asleep on the floor.

All of us can probably recall similar incidents from our own experience in which stimulation was misperceived and distorted as a result of motivational or emotional factors. An interesting example of such effects on a large population of individuals is the recent and reoccurring reports of unidentified flying objects. During the past ten or fifteen years there have been numerous reports from individuals throughout the country who claim to have seen aircraft of odd shapes, usually circular, that travel at fantastic speeds and are presumed to represent "invaders" from other planets. There have even been reports of landings, after which strange-looking creatures have been said to emerge. Such reports not only are numerous, numbering in the thousands, but are taken as serious evidence of the existence of higher forms of life and of an advanced space technology on other planets. Naturally the veracity of these observations is a matter of grave concern; if true, the implications for our national security, to say nothing of our space program, would be revolutionary.

Based on analysis of such reports from untrained volunteeer observers, one cannot state with certainty that such spacecraft do or do not exist. However, one can examine the reports within the context of our knowledge of visual perception to determine what bases may exist for the observations. Because the perceptual system of the human observer is by no means infallible, it is possible that some of the reports may be "explained" as misinterpretations based on fear, lack of knowledge, social pressures, or expectations. For example, the misinterpretation of the exhaust from jet aircraft, the reflection of sun from an airplane, and various meteorological phenomena, it is felt, could well be the bases for many of the reports of unidentified flying objects. In addition, there are a number of factors within the structure of the eye itself that might be responsible. We know that the humors of the eye, the fluids inside the eyeball, contain imperfections that can cast shadows on the retina. We also know that under conditions in which one observes a uniform surface, such as the sky, these shadows as well as blood cells that are continually passing in front of the retina may become visible. These can be noticed by staring at a blank sheet of paper that is strongly illuminated. The observer who is unaware of these phenomena, and by virtue of his curiosity, fear, or social pressure is "looking for" flying saucers or other strange aircraft, may well misinterpret these ambiguous stimuli. It is understandable that what one perceives under these conditions might be misinterpreted to be what one is actually expecting to see. It is not claimed that all such reports are false. Rather, the point to be made here is simply that a knowledge of visual perception and of the effect of motivation requires us *first* to consider the strong possibility that the reports have much simpler explanations before assuming that we are being invaded by creatures from outer space.

In some instances, such as those described above, the effect of motivation on perception is undesirable, because it decreases the reliability of the observer (Poffenberger, 1942). In the field of law the unreliability of observers is notorious and poses a major problem in the courts. If there are ten witnesses to an accident, the ten reports will probably differ significantly. In fact, if you ask a number of observers to look at a photograph, say from a magazine, the variability of their reports will be amazingly high.

On the positive side, it is possible to take advantage of this variability in perception in order to tell us something about the individual. In the assessment of individual differences and personality, an attempt has been made to provide subjects with ambiguous stimuli, assuming that the reports given will reflect meaningful aspects of the observer's personality. Perhaps the best known of the "projective" techniques is the Rorschach ink-blot test. This test consists of a series of figures that have literally been made by ink blots. The subject is shown the ink blots and asked to describe what he sees. It is assumed that because he is objectively looking at an ink blot, what he reports must, of necessity, reflect his own motives, needs, desires, and so on. The stimulus itself is said to be "unstructured" and is chosen to produce no definite response on the part of the subject. The Rorschach test has been used extensively as a method for differentiating among individuals and for assessing personality. At the present time some serious problems exist regarding the scoring and interpretation of this test. However, it and other projective techniques have a reasonable basis in the known effects of motivation on perception (Lindzey, 1961). There is no question that some relationship between these variables exists. Ambiguous stimuli can evoke responses that have their origin in the personality structure of the observer. The practical problem is one of devising a satisfactory method of scoring and interpreting these responses.

A relatively large portion of the literature in this field has been concerned with the effects of perception on needs and wants. Psychologists have shown experimentally that the perceived size of postage stamps and other objects depends upon their monetary value. There is some indication that the perceived size of coins by children depends upon their needs. It has been claimed that "wealthy" children will perceive the same coin as being smaller than will a "poor" child of the same age. (See Woodworth & Schlosberg, 1954.) An interesting extension of this line of investigation has been the influence of prestige on perceived size. For a young child the size of an individual is of great importance. To a first grader a third-grade student is a very strong and powerful person. This is reflected in the language of the young child, who often associates size with strength and power. It is not unusual for a youngster to overestimate the size of someone who is in a position of authority—for example, his school principal—or to underestimate the size of another adult who is not viewed as an authority or power figure. This hypothesis has been tested by a Belgian psychologist, Jacques Bude, who demonstrated that those individuals in a group of boys who are strong and dominant are perceived as taller than those boys who are less strong and dominant (Bude, 1960). We know, of course, that perceived size is by no means a simple matter. Rather, it is influenced by context, by experience, and in the present case by the "value" ascribed to it by the observer.

Perhaps the most extreme example that one can find of the effect of motivation on perception is the dramatic distortions of perception that take place as a result of hypnosis. Under the hypnotic trance, which can be viewed as experimentally induced motivation, our perceptions can undergo all sorts of predictable alterations. Water can be made to "taste" like champagne, like a bitter fluid, or like any other substance suggested by the hypnotist. A pencil point placed gently on the skin may be perceived as sharp, hot, or cold. We know of course that hypnosis is only an extreme form of suggestion and that suggestive influences operate subtly and commonly in everyday life. Indeed, the untrained human being is not a very good observer of complex perceptual events. The realization of this fact is not only important in law and science, but in our personal lives as well. If we admit the possibility that people can honestly give different reports of the same objective scenes, we will have made a significant step toward the understanding of one of the basic facts about human behavior.

The effect of motivation on perception is well illustrated in the paper by Leuba and Lucas. [4] [2] By using hypnosis, which may be considered as experimentally induced motivation or attitude formation, the same picture evoked significantly different responses, depending upon the attitude induced by the hypnotist. It is fortunate indeed when everyday experience and laboratory experimentation lead to the same conclusions.

The subtle example of the influence of motivation on perception was demonstrated accidentally in relation to experiments on distorted rooms. It is possible to build a room that, although not rectangular, appears so to the observer. This is accomplished by constructing the room as indicated in Figure 3. The dimensions of the room, however, are carefully calculated so that from the point of view of an observer looking into the room from the position indicated, the room appears normal. If, however, we place individuals in the windows of the room, they will appear grossly distorted in size. This room, devised by Dr. Adelbert Ames, was used extensively on research in perception at Princeton University (Ittleson & Kilpatrick, 1951). Most individuals looking at such a room will report that the room looks normal, but the individuals appear to be different in size. However, Dr. Warren Wittreich [5], working at Princeton in one of these rooms, discovered that when one of the faces bears a "special relationship" to the observer, such as a fiance or wife, the faces are perceived as normal and the room distorted. In other words, the conflict regarding whether the face or the room is normal, although usually resolved in favor of a normal room and an abnormally sized face, is seen under special conditions of motivation to be resolved in the opposite direction.

[2] Bracketed numbers refer to readings in Part Two.

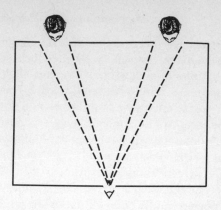

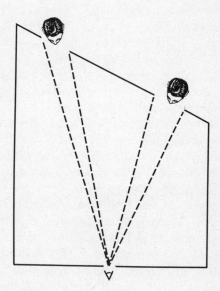

FIGURE 3. Schematic diagram comparing a normal room (upper) with a distorted room (lower). In the normal room, the windows are the same size. In the lower room, the left window, which is farther away, has purposely been made bigger than the right window. As a result of the perspective design of the room, both windows appear, from the indicated observation position, to be the same size. However, a human head in each window under normal circumstances will appear relatively smaller on the left, both because it is farther away and because it is framed by a larger window.

This phenomenon has been called the "Honi" effect, because it was first observed by an especially devoted couple, one of whom was nicknamed "Honi." It illustrates the fact that perception and perceptual compromise are strongly affected by motivational variables. The very simple comment that "we see what we want to see" and do not see what we do not want to see has a firm basis in experience and laboratory experimentation. The Honi effect demonstrates experimentally the phenomenon that is implied by the familiar statement "love is blind." In this context, of course, it would be more correct to say that love affects perception, but the end result and meaning are the same in both cases.

VI

Illusions: The Fallibility
of Perception

PREVIOUS CHAPTERS HAVE POINTED OUT THAT SUBSE-
quent to stimulation of the eye by light, a number of transformations
take place before awareness occurs. In general, these transformations
are in the interest of the biological adjustment of the organism in
that the end result is a correct or true perception of the external
world. Occasionally perceptions take place that are incorrect, the
true state of the environment being misperceived. Such incorrect
perceptions are referred to as illusions and are perfectly normal
experiences. In Figure 4 and on page 81 are illustrated some
examples of illusions such as usually appear in elementary textbooks.
(For a more extensive presentation see Luckiesch, 1922.) Typically
illusions are merely presented as demonstrations, with no attempt
to explain their origin or significance.

From a scientific point of view, an unexplained illusion represents
an undesirable state of affairs. The same perceptual system that
operates in everyday life must, of necessity, be set into action when
observing an illusion. Logically, an illusion represents much more
than an anomaly and should, more correctly, be considered an indication that our knowledge of fundamental laws of perception is
inadequate. Illusions, in this context, can serve as guideposts indi-

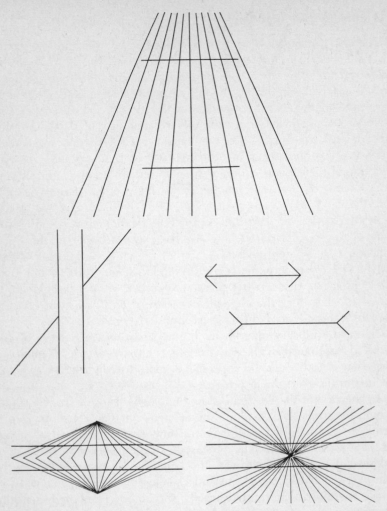

FIGURE 4. Some examples of optical illusions. *Top:* The illusion of Ponzo. Are the two horizontal lines of equal length? *Middle, left:* If the lower half of the diagonal were extended, would it meet the upper half? *Middle, right:* Are the two horizontal lines of equal length? *Bottom:* Are the pairs of horizontal lines parallel?

cating in which direction future research in perception should be aimed.

This point of view has been well illustrated by the German physiologist Erich von Holst (von Holst, 1957). He argues that the basic structure of many illusions can be identified in everyday perception. Consider as an example the illusion illustrated in Figure 4, usually referred to as the illusion of Ponzo. The horizontal lines are drawn to be of equal length, but the one nearer the open end of the figure appears smaller than the one nearer the closed end. It is interesting to note that knowledge of the objective equality of these lines does not destroy the illusion. On the contrary, if the reader will actually measure the lines so as to be convinced of their equality, his perception of their length will nevertheless remain unequal and illusory. In general, illusions are unaffected by knowledge of the true state of affairs.

How can one explain this compelling phenomenon? In Figure 5 von Holst has illustrated how the basic components of the Ponzo illusion can be identified in a familiar viewing situation. We have all had frequent experiences with similar scenes during our lives. In comparing these two figures we have a vivid example of the point of view that the elements of illusory figures are in fact, the figures themselves, familiar perceptual experiences. Therefore in viewing the illusory diagram in Figure 4 we will make use of perceptual mechanisms that have a long history of use in our past experience and would be expected to manifest themselves as active factors in the perceptual process.

In the case of the Ponzo illusion, the mechanisms of size constancy would be applicable. It would be argued that size constancy represents a "correction" for the diminishing size of the retinal image as the distance of objects is increased. A potent indicator of distance is the convergence of straight lines such as are represented by the sides of the road in our illustration, telephone wires, the walls of rooms and corridors, railroad tracks, and so on. The convergence of lines serves as an indicator of distance and implies that the observer should make a "correction" by increasing the subjective size of distant objects. This correction would compensate for the decrease in retinal image size that normally occurs when distance is increased and would result in a more true perception of the environment. This mechanism serves an important and appropriate role in everyday vision in helping to produce the size constancy effect. However, when the same elements are taken out of context and presented in an illusory figure, the effect of correction for the diminishing retinal image size of distantly located objects is brought into play inappropriately and results in an illusory experience. What we have here is a perceptual mechanism appropriate to normal viewing but producing an incorrect perceptual experience in an artificial viewing situation. Thus the illusion should not be considered merely as an anomaly, but rather as the misapplication of one of the mechanisms of size constancy.

FIGURE 5. Sketch by von Holst illustrating the similarity between the illusion of Ponzo and a typical scene from everyday life. Are the two horizontal logs of the same length? (After E. von Holst, *Studium Generale*, Vol. 10, pp. 231–243 (1957), Springer-Verlag, Berlin, Göttingen, Heidelberg. Used by permission.)

As a test of this hypothesis the author investigated the development of size constancy as well as the magnitude of the Ponzo illusion in children of various ages. In confirmation of the assumption that they have a common origin, it was discovered that both size constancy for distant objects and the Ponzo illusion increase with age at a similar rate. Furthermore, neither is affected by intellectual level or education, pointing to the important role played by experience in the development of their common mechanism (Leibowitz and Heisel, 1958).

A dramatic example of the role played by illusions in focusing the attention of psychologists on important relationships occurred in the early part of this century with respect to the illusion of apparent motion. If two lights are flashed intermittently at various rates, a speed of alternation will be reached at which the two lights, instead of appearing to flash on and off, which is the true state of affairs, will appear to move back and forth between their respective locations. This is the illusion of apparent motion with which we are all familiar by virtue of its applications in advertising signs and motion pictures (Kolers, 1964). In the case of the motion pictures, the rapid flashing of successive photographs at the correct rate produces an illusion of motion that is so real that it has provided the basis for both the motion picture and television industries.

In the early part of this century the German psychologist Max Wertheimer became interested in explaining the apparent motion illusion. For Wertheimer the problem was important not only because of his interest in the illusion per se, but because the theoretical framework provided by many of his contemporaries seemed to him to exclude the possibility that the illusion should even exist! During this period the psychological school of structuralism, which argued that one should study the elements of experience, was in vogue. In the case of the apparent motion illusion this approach failed to suggest an explanation, because the elements were simply two flashing lights. Thus the apparent motion represents an aspect of experience that is *not* in the elements of stimulation and must, according to Wertheimer, be supplied by the observer. This approach, stressing the contribution of the observer to perception, led to the development of the Gestalt school of psychology in opposition to the then popular structuralism. The gestaltists have contributed immensely to our knowledge and understanding of perception by analyzing the ways in which the organization of mental processes shape and influence perceptual experience. It is unfortunately not possible to elaborate on their specific contributions in this essay. However, it is important to note that this historic and fruitful approach to the problems of psychology was initiated by the discrepancy between the illusion of apparent motion and the then contemporary knowledge and methods of approach in the study of visual perception (Woodworth & Sheehan, 1964).

Although all of the many illusions identified to date have not played such an important role in the history of psychology, it is clear that the scientific study of illusions is not only interesting but profitable. In the field of perception, several illusions have been explained in terms of normal mechanisms, for example, the Ponzo illusion. Other illusions have stimulated research directed toward the identification of such mechanisms. Of particular interest is the study of the moon illusion, which results from the fact that the moon appears larger near the horizon than it does when viewed higher in the heavens. It has been estimated that the moon, under ideal observation conditions, appears two or three times larger at the horizon than when viewed overhead. This is an incorrect perception, because the moon does not change size as it rises. Strictly speaking, it should appear somewhat larger when it rises because the overhead moon is actually slightly closer to the observer than when it is viewed near the horizon. The larger apparent size of the horizon moon is probably the oldest illusion observed, having been discussed in early Greek and Roman literature. Tracing the history of this illusion is a fascinating experience, because an unusually wide variety of individuals have been challenged to offer an explanation.

The explanations offered are numerous and varied. It has been suggested that because the horizon moon can be compared with familiar objects on the ground, it appears larger by contrast with terrestrial objects than the overhead moon, which is viewed alone. The fact that the horizon moon is seen through more atmosphere, and appears redder, has been offered. Other explanations include the position of the eyes in the head, the asymmetry of perceived space, and the differential development of size constancy in the horizontal and vertical directions.

The paper by Rock and Kaufman [6] [1] represents a recent attack on this compelling and persistent illusion by means of a novel experimental approach. They conclude that the crucial variable is the presence or absence of terrain that would be visible when observing the moon at the horizon but that would not be as conspicuous when looking at the moon higher in the sky. As Rock and

[1] Bracketed numbers refer to readings in Part Two.

Kaufman point out, however, they are at a loss to explain the results of Boring's experiments, in which the illusion was attributed to the elevation of the eyes when observing the overhead moon (Boring, 1943). Although variations in conclusions between competent investigators may seem contradictory, it should be pointed out that there were significant differences in apparatus and procedure in the two studies that could conceivably account for the discordant results. In every experimental situation there is always the risk that the particular experimental apparatus or procedure may contribute to the results obtained. It is only by the scientific procedure of continually checking and cross-checking experimental conclusions found by different investigators that the correct results are finally obtained.

With respect to the moon illusion, a more complete understanding of the basis for the effect as well as the resolution of the many conflicts among competent investigators will be forthcoming when our knowledge of size, space, and distance perception and of size constancy has advanced sufficiently to treat the illusion as a special case of these more general phenomena (Boring, 1942). It may well turn out to be the case that there are a number of variables that might contribute to the moon illusion effect under different conditions. The nature of biological systems is seldom simple.

Our brief treatment of perceptual illusions is intended in part as an object lesson in the philosophy of science. A number of years ago a physician discovered an outbreak of a disease that was thought to have disappeared in modern hospitals when antiseptic conditions were introduced. His assistants were deeply embarrassed, because the mere presence of this disease was an indication that the hospital had been grossly negligent. They advised their chief to "cover up" the disease so that the chief and the hospital would not be publicly embarrassed. The head physician refused, stating that because the disease had never before appeared in a modern hospital, here was an opportunity to study it scientifically. The physician eventually became one of the outstanding members of his profession. His attitude toward the disease is equally applicable to the study of visual illusions. A serious student of perception should be embarrassed by their presence. If, however, they are viewed as challenging phenomena, the explanation of which will advance the state of the art in this field, their recognition can serve a most salutary purpose. The strength of the effort to better understand illusions will serve as an indicator of the level of maturity in the scientific study of visual perception.

VII

Perception in Modern Technology

LEST THE READER ASSUME THAT PERCEPTION IS PRImarily an academic topic, it should be pointed out that a knowledge of perception and perceptual capacities can play an important role in modern technology. Consider, for example, the effect of the development of ever more rapid means of transportation. A human being walks at a speed of approximately four miles per hour. At this speed two human beings approaching each other have adequate time to change their direction and avoid collision. It is a rare event when pedestrians collide even in our busy modern cities. Human perception, assuming normal vision and attention, is fast enough under these circumstances to give warning to the individuals and permit adequate time for evasive action. In a modern motor vehicle the demands placed on the human being are more stringent. Assume two automobiles are approaching each other at a speed of 60 miles per hour (88 feet per second) each. Under daylight illumination conditions the *minimum* time required for the drivers to sense danger ahead and to alter the course of their vehicles would be about 0.2 second. This is called the reaction time and results from the time required for the eye, brain, and muscles to react. This 0.2 second is a minimum figure; lower illumination levels, increasing age of the driver, time required to make a decision, fatigue, and many other factors increase this duration so that under most conditions a more reasonable minimum reaction time would be about 0.5 second. This reaction time does not include time required for the vehicle itself to be altered by changing direction or stopping. It merely refers to the time required from the instant the light rays strike the eye until the muscles controlling the vehicle are energized. The greater part of this total reaction time consists of the time necessary for the perception of the situation. During this half-second interval, our two cars approaching each other at 60 miles per hour will have closed the distance between them by 88 feet. This means that the perceptual system of the human beings involved in these automobiles is essentially useless for emergencies that arise within the limitations of human reaction time. If two cars traveling at 60 miles per hour and heading toward each other first become visible when the distance between them is 88 feet or less, a crash is inevitable. By the time the drivers can begin to turn their wheels or apply the brakes, the collision will have occurred. Motor vehicle specialists are very much aware of the importance of reaction time, and advise drivers to allow an adequate safety margin to compensate for the limitations placed on human driving ability by reaction time and the time required to brake or alter the course of the vehicle.

If we look at even more rapid means of transportation, the time to perceive danger and to react becomes increasingly critical. The pilots of two airplanes approaching each other at 600 miles per hour will have closed the gap between them by a distance of 880 feet during the half-second reaction time. As planes travel at even greater speeds, such as the supersonic transports now on the drawing boards, the problem is magnified proportionately. Two planes traveling at three times the speed of sound will have diminished the distance between them by over a half mile during the half-second reaction time period. An orbiting astronaut, moving at 18,000 miles per hour, will travel approximately two and half miles during one half second. Despite dramatic advances in technology, human perception time remains unchanged and acts as a factor limiting the usefulness of the human operator.

One may well ask at this point why human beings are used at all in these situations when the slowness of the perceptual system poses such problems. In modern technology there have been, in fact, many successful attempts to replace the human being with more efficient mechanical systems. Radar permits airplane pilots to be aware of objects many miles beyond the limitations of human perception and to do so under adverse weather conditions. Radar can function at night or in fog when a human being would be essentially "blind." Radar, automatic warning systems, photocells, and so on, are in many applications faster, cheaper, and more reliable than if the same job were performed by a human being.

However, there are many tasks for which it is not feasible to replace the human being with automatic equipment. An historic example occurred during the Mercury Orbital Flight of astronaut Gordon Cooper in May, 1963. Although the Mercury system was designed to permit automatic reentry into the earth's atmosphere, difficulties arose that required astronaut Cooper to orient his spacecraft manually prior to reentry and landing. Without the perceptual and motor capacities of the human being, it would not have been possible to bring the spacecraft safely back to earth. With Cooper available to supplement the automated equipment, the Mercury capsule was recovered only two miles from the planned impact point! A most remarkable and historic event! (See Mercury Project Summary, 1963.)

A more commonplace example occurs in the piloting of aircraft. Although much of the flight of an airplane can be automated, there is still considerable doubt that one can trust to machines the complex maneuvering required during the approach and landing in a busy airport (Brady, F. B., 1964). The problem here is that one can build a machine directed to perform under optimum conditions in a reliable, rigid way. However, when unexpected contingencies arise, the flexibility of the human being is invaluable.

It is interesting to analyze the kinds of perceptual tasks for which the presence of the human being seems to be essential and for which no satisfactory automated substitute has yet been found. Machines are extremely efficient at simple jobs such as counting. If one wanted to know the number of individuals who passed a certain place— for example, through the door of a store—it would be a very simple matter to set up a photoelectric system that would count the number of times a human being passed a certain point. The automatic system would do an excellent job under these conditions. If necessary, one could also devise such a system to tell us how tall the people are, how fast they walk through the door, or how much they weigh. If, however, we wish to know how many are males and how many are females, the job becomes impossibly complex for a machine, but, of course, remains a very simple task for a human being. The principle here is that a well-defined repetitive task is easily handled by machines. More complex perceptual tasks that present many different alternatives are extremely difficult to automate, but remain relatively simple for human beings.

The problem of when to assign a task to a machine or to a human being, or more commonly what part of a task to assign to a human being and to a machine, is the job for a member of the relatively young discipline referred to as human engineering, engineering psychology, or human factors. Individuals in this field evaluate the roles played by men and machines and, based on a knowledge of the limitations and capabilities of both, make assignments accordingly (Sinaiko, 1961). A significant portion of their work involves a knowledge of perception. For example, the task very frequently assigned to the human operator, such as an airplane pilot, is the reading of dials and gauges. In order to maximize the contribution of the human being in this situation, the human engineer takes into account his perceptual capacities and attempts to design the indicator so as to eliminate errors, avoid confusion, and maximize the efficiency of the man-machine combination (Chapanis, 1953).

The paper by Professor S. S. Stevens [7] [1] of Harvard University, written shortly after the end of World War II, described some of the human engineering problems faced by our military services during this conflict and the attempts by Professor Stevens' laboratory to contribute to their solution through experimental psychology. Psychologists are proud of their contributions, both military and nonmilitary, to our modern technology made through their efforts to effect ever more efficient use of the man-machine combination. Fortunately Professor Stevens' warning that experimental psychology should not ignore the problems of the military during peacetime was heeded. There are a number of active laboratories in operation today that seek to improve our knowledge of men and machines

---

[1] Bracketed numbers refer to readings in Part Two.

both in the interest of keeping the peace and in an attempt to expand our basic knowledge of the human being.

There has been serious thought given to the problem regarding the role to be played by the astronaut and his human perceptual capacities in our future space program. One function, of course, is as a "back-up" system, which, as in the case of astronaut Cooper's historic flight, would take over when automatic equipment failed. There are, however, other functions that will most probably depend heavily on the skills of the human being. For example, the rendezvous of two vehicles in orbit, a maneuver planned as part of the moon exploration program, will prove to be most challenging from the point of view of technology. It will be necessary for the astronaut to position his spacecraft so as to approach another spacecraft while both are traveling at a speed of about 5 miles per second. The ability of the human to estimate distance and to operate his controls so as to achieve the precise positioning necessary will place great demands on his perceptual system. Our basic knowledge of perception in the normal earth environment will be helpful in making predictions about perception in space. However, the unusual environmental conditions involved in space flight may require additional information as to the effect of space travel on perceptual capabilities (Brown, 1964).

The problem facing the human engineer has been most succinctly stated by Robert Boynton of the University of Rochester, who, while noting that we are now in a period characterized by phenomenal advances in electronic sensors, stated: "Everyday, it seems, we hear of further progress and refinements; equipment is becoming more compact, more versatile. However, we must admit that no one is ever going to redesign the human eye, so all we can do is to determine its capabilities and learn to use it more effectively." [2] It should be added that the success with which we accomplish this task determines, in no insignificant way, the rate of advance of our automated technology, the success or failure of our space program, and the efficiency of our military establishment. Perhaps in the catastrophic event of a national emergency the survival of our way

[2] Ailene Morris and E. Porter Horne, *Visual Search Techniques* (Washington, D.C.: National Academy of Sciences, National Research Council, 1960), p. v.

of life may be at stake. Walter Hunter, the late distinguished experimental psychologist from Brown University, has stated our
task simply and effectively:

> Should another war come, victory may well be, not on the side of the
> strongest battalions, not even on the side of the best guided missiles, but
> on the side which has gained a vital 10 percent in the successful handling
> of human factors problems.[3]

[3] *Human Factors in Underseas Warfare* (Washington, D.C.: National Research Council, Committee on Underseas Warfare, 1949), p. viii.

CHAPTER VIII

Perception and the Nervous System

IN THE HISTORY OF PSYCHOLOGY MUCH EFFORT HAS BEEN directed toward identifying the role that the nervous system plays in behavior and experience. These inquiries have included the problem of visual perception. One of the pioneer investigators in studying the relationship between the nervous system and perception is Lord Adrian of Cambridge University in England (Adrian, 1928, 1947). Lord Adrian demonstrated that the units of the nervous system, the individual nerve fibers, do not respond continuously when activated, but rather give off a series of sharp electrical discharges or "spikes," as illustrated in Figure 6. As the strength of the stimulus is increased, the effect on the individual cells is to increase the frequency of these discharges. However, there is a limit to the speed at which an individual element can be activated, the maximum being of the order of 1,000 spikes per second. Under no condition is it found that the individual cells respond continuously.

This raises the question as to how perceptual experience can be continuous when the elements that form the basis of perception are responding essentially discontinuously. The answer is relatively simple. The individual nerve fiber response illustrated in the figure is obtained by isolating a single nerve cell either surgically or mechanically. In the intact nervous system, we have literally thousands of such nerve fibers responding together. Thus the continuity of perception is based on the combined action of many individual nerve cells. If this were not the case, the world would look, as Adrian has pointed out, as if we were viewing it from a moving automobile through a picket fence. The importance of considering the combined action of individual nerve fibers has stimulated much work in the neurophysiology of perception. Let us consider as an example a classical problem in perception for which valuable information has been recently supplied by such studies.

The human eye, in terms of its optical qualities, is very poor indeed. Helmholtz has stated that if an optician wanted to sell him an optical instrument that had as many defects as the human eye, he would be justified in strongly reprimanding the optician and returning his instrument (Helmholtz, 1962b). In an ideal optical instrument rays from a point source are focused at a corresponding point on the retina of the eye. This condition is *never* attained in living eyes. Rather, the more typical situation is one in which the rays from the object point are imaged over a fairly wide area. The failure of light rays from object points to meet in a common image point is referred to as the aberration of the eye. As an example of the problem raised by the presence of aberrations in the eye, Figure 7 (top) illustrates the ideal light intensity at the edge of a black line, such as one might see in reading black print, on a white background. Instead of the rectangular distribution of light, as illustrated by the theoretical curve at the top of the figure, one obtains spreading of the light at the borders, as indicated by the center curve. It would be natural to expect from this analysis that the border should appear fuzzy and not distinct and sharp as we know is the case in everyday life. For many years, students of visual perception have attempted to explain this paradox. Recently Drs. F. Ratliff and H. K. Hartline of the Rockefeller Institute have demonstrated a mechanism whereby the nervous system essentially "corrects" for the imperfections of the retinal image (Ratliff & Hartline, 1959). The lower diagram of Figure 7 illustrates the recorded frequency of nerve impulses from single fibers of the eye of the horseshoe crab *Limulus* in response to stimulation by the light distribution produced by a border. Recalling that the frequency of discharge of the nerve fibers is the determiner of perceived intensity, it is interesting to note that the differences in light intensity which exist in the retinal image are actually exag-

58 *Inquiry and Argument*

gerated by the nervous mechanism of the intact eye. The fuzzy retinal image is actually "sharpened" and corrected by the nervous system. The mechanism by which this sharpening takes place is that of contrast. Each sensory cell exerts an inhibitory effect on every other cell and is in turn inhibited by every other activated cell. For the cells at the lighter edge of the retinal image, the net effect of stimulating the entire eye is to diminish the inhibitory

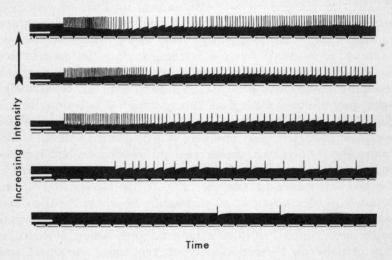

Time

FIGURE 6. Records of the electrical "spike" potentials from single fibers of the eye of the horseshoe crab, *Limulus*. Successively higher records on the diagram have been produced by increasing levels of light intensity. The white interrupted line at the bottom of each record indicates time in ⅕ second. The steady white line at the left indicates the period of illumination. Note the discontinuous character of the responses even at the highest level of intensity. (After Hartline, H. K. Cold Spring Harbor Symposium on Quantitative Biology, 1935. Used by permission.)

effects on them coming from the darker portion of the image. This release from inhibition results in an increase in discharge frequency. The opposite effect takes place at the dark edge of the image. The net result of the interaction is to increase the contrast between the light and the dark edge of the image and render it more like that situation that would prevail if the eye did not suffer so severely from optical aberrations. Thus the optical defects of the eye are minimized by the nervous interaction among the visual sense cells.

Although Ratliff and Hartline were studying extremely primitive eyes, there is ample evidence to support the point of view that this mechanism of interaction, referred to as contrast, is typical of all species. Thus the interplay of sense cells compensates for the imperfections of the optical system of the eye and produces perceptions that are more in accord with reality than we would expect, knowing that our retinal image is blurred. The results of Ratliff and Hartline are classic, and have gone a long way toward explaining one of the oldest and most troublesome problems of visual perception.

There are other types of aberrations that do not fit the model of Ratliff and Hartline. For example, we know that the eye is not corrected for chromatic aberration. The retinal image of a point, besides being blurred by various types of geometrical aberrations, should also be colored, because the eye is not capable of focusing the various colors of light components precisely at the same retinal image point. Thus a prediction based on optics would suggest that the edges of all light objects should appear colored like the rainbow. We know that such a condition simply does not exist. The method by which this chromatic error is eliminated is not well understood, but it does seem to depend upon experience. This conclusion is based on the observation that if human beings wear glasses, either experimentally or to correct faulty eyesight, color fringes are produced temporarily but in time simply disappear. This disappearance is complete within several days. Interestingly enough, when the glasses are removed, the subject sees colors that are the opposite of those he observed when he first put on the glasses. Thus it would appear that the nervous system somehow "adapts" to unwanted color fringes by building up an opposing response that cancels them out (Kohler, 1962).

The results of the experiments on individual nerve cell activity and the cancellation of color fringes both indicate that the nervous system is definitely not a passive receiver of stimuli. On the contrary, the nervous system reacts actively and modifies the excitations produced by light in predictable ways. The German physiologist von Holst has pointed out another interesting example of the way in which the nervous system serves actively to modify visual perception. Among insects there are a number of examples of responses

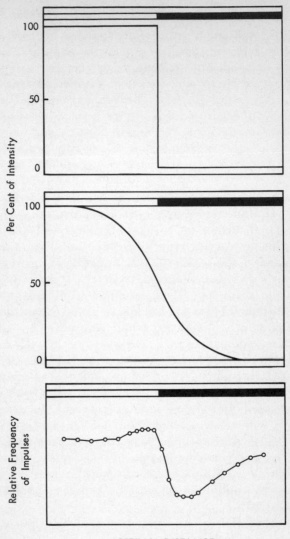

FIGURE 7. *Upper diagram:* The hypothetical distribution of light intensity in the retinal image of a white edge on a black background in the absence of aberrations and diffraction. *Middle:* Calculated distribution of light intensity taking aberrations and diffraction into account. (From "The Relation Between Visual Acuity and Illumination" by Simon Schlaer. Reprinted by permission of The Rockefeller Institute Press, from *Journal of General Physiology,* 1937, Vol. 21, No. 2, p. 178.) *Bottom:* Frequency of nerve impulses in the eye of the horseshoe crab, *Limulus,* as a function of retinal distance when the entire

that follow automatically upon the application of a stimulus. The dragon fly *Eristalis* shows such a response when it is placed in a drum lined with vertical black and white stripes. As the drum is rotated, the fly "follows" the movement of the stripes. It is "as if" the nervous system of the animal were "locked in" to the movement of his environment. Many animals exhibit such innate reflex activity. However, the reflex nature of this response raises an interesting question. If movement of the stripes forces the animal to respond by moving in the same direction, what is the result when the animal itself moves its body? When the animal moves, there is motion of the stripes in the eye of the animal, a condition that should evoke the reflex response. Obviously, as von Holst has pointed out, the animal is able to distinguish between movement of the stripes in his eye produced by itself from that produced by external motion. Although the nerve impulses traveling from the eye to the brain are the same in both cases, the brain is able to make a distinction as to the source of the motion. The ability to make this distinction is indeed a very important one for living organisms at all levels. An old problem in human visual perception is to explain why we do not perceive motion of our environment when we move our eyes. In glancing first at the left side of this book and then at the right, the book does not appear to move, although the movement of the eyes in their sockets produces motion of the retinal image. On the other hand, if we move a book with our arms, or someone else moves it, motion is perceived. In both cases, the movement of the retinal image is similar, and we may assume that the impulses traveling along the optic nerves are also similar. The fact that we do not perceive motion when it is self-produced is analogous to the situation of the fly in the center of the striped drum. Von Holst has suggested that we are able, by means of unconscious mechanisms, to anticipate self-produced motion so that the resulting impulses produced are actually canceled somewhere in the brain.

---

eye is illuminated. Note the exaggeration of the bright and dark portions as a result of contrast. (From "The Response of *Limulus* Optic Nerve Fibers to Patterns of Illumination on the Receptor Mosaic" by F. Ratliff and H. K. Hartline. Reprinted by permission of The Rockefeller Institute Press, from *Journal of General Physiology*, 1959, Vol. 42, No. 6, p. 1248.)

The reprint by the late Professon von Holst [8] [1] describes the experiments with the dragon fly and introduces the important concept that the central nervous system must be able to differentiate stimulation produced by self-initiated movement of the sense organs (reafference) from stimulation of a passive sense organ by external forces (exafference). As a biologist interested in the relations between the central nervous system and the peripheral organs, Professor von Holst applied this differentiation successfully to a number of perceptual problems. This principle of reafference has been extended to problems different from those described here. In particular, Richard Held [3] has hypothesized that reafference is necessary for the relearning of sensory motor coordination. At the present time it is too early to assess the ultimate contribution of the concept of reafference to perception and perceptual learning. It is, however, a reasonable concept that is at least consistent with behavioral data on the following reflex of the dragon fly, position constancy in humans, the sensory effect of paralysis of the eye muscles, and size constancy. An appealing aspect of this principle is its wide applicability; although it was first conceived by von Holst in connection with motor coordination of the spinal cord, it is seen to be applicable to species as diverse as insects, fish, and humans and to motor coordination, and perceptual and perceptual-motor learning phenomena.

The importance of these studies can perhaps best be appreciated from the historical point of view. In the early attempts to understand behavior and experience, the pioneers in psychology approached the task within the framework of their day, which included heavy emphasis on and respect for the structure or anatomy of the nervous system. Their thinking was influenced by the orderly arrangement of nerve fibers and other aspects of the body, and their theories were obviously influenced by anatomical facts and principles. Later in the history of neurophysiology, when electrical recording techniques became possible, studies such as those by Adrian and Hartline pointed out that the nervous system does not simply receive stimuli but rather acts in a positive way to modify excitation before awareness takes place. These studies, and especially the essay by

---

[1] Bracketed numbers refer to readings in Part Two.

von Holst, illustrate how our thinking has changed during the past century from that of a passive, atomistic, mechanical nervous system to one that is active. One may say that the nervous system serves as a background against which incoming stimuli are evaluated, modified, and finally perceived.

The point of view that the nervous system actively contributes to and modifies perception is a fitting epilogue for this essay. It was pointed out in Chapter I that perception is adaptive, that stimulation is modified in the interest of the stability and continuity of perceptual experience. In Chapters III and V examples of learned and motivational factors were enumerated. Chapter VI on illusions represents a mismodification, but nevertheless an active change in stimulation by a "nonpassive nervous system." All of these chapters share in common examples of the active role of the organism in perception, some physiological mechanisms of which are illustrated in this final chapter. Because the goal of science is prediction, and such prediction is based on the application to novel situations of well-established principles, it would appear to the writer that the implied principle of active modification of stimulation by the organism is a most valuable concept to consider when thinking about or predicting perceptual experience. Consider what we would perceive if we "saw" the blurred, colored, and rapidly changing physical characteristics of our fuzzy retinal images. The results would be chaotic, and our vision would be, if not completely useless, much less efficient than is now the case. The study of how the organism modifies this retinal image to produce the splendidly organized perceptual world of experience defines a fruitful approach to the study of perception.

PART TWO

The Selected Readings

IMPORTANT SOURCES INCLUDED IN WHOLE OR IN PART

[1] E. G. Boring, "The Perception of Objects"

[2] H. P. Zeigler and H. W. Leibowitz, "Apparent Visual Size as a Function of Distance for Children and Adults"

[3] R. Held and M. Schlank, "Adaptation to Disarranged Eye-Hand Coordination in the Distance-Dimension"

[4] C. Leuba and C. Lucas, "The Effects of Attitudes on Descriptions of Pictures"

[5] W. J. Wittreich, "The Honi Phenomenon: A Case of Selective Perceptual Distortion"

[6] I. Rock and L. Kaufman, "The Moon Illusion, II"

[7] S. S. Stevens, "Machines Cannot Fight Alone"

[8] E. von Holst, "Relations Between the Central Nervous System and the Peripheral Organs"

[1]
The Perception of Objects

EDWIN G. BORING

For more than a century it has been customary to say that perception is something more than sensory impression, that perception is *of an object,* that it corresponds to a stimulating object. The modern view is that, because objects are permanent, a perception of an object tends to remain constant even when the immediate sensory impressions upon which the perception is based vary with the variety of conditions that affect stimulation.

This general rule of perception applies to all sense departments. It depends upon an integrative property of the brain and is not a function of sense organs at all. The meaning of the rule is most easily expounded in terms of particular instances, and the four examples that are best understood are the visual perception of size with distance variant, of shape with angle of regard variant, of brightness with intensity of illumination variant, and of hue with color of illumination variant.[1]

We know a great deal about perceived *size* with distance variant. At short distances perceived size tends not to change with distance. A man is 40 feet down the hall and walking toward you. When he is only 20 feet away, has he doubled his height? The height of the

---

[1] On constancy in the perception of objects, see, for elementary accounts, E. G. Boring, H. S. Langfeld and H. P. Weld, *Introduction to Psychology* (New York: Wiley, 1939), pp. 420–427, 463f., 468f.; R. S. Woodworth, *Experimental Psychology* (New York: Holt, 1938), pp. 595–622. Another summary of the facts with historical orientation and two score references is in E. G. Boring, *Sensation and Perception in the History of Experimental Psychology* (New York: Appleton-Century, 1942), pp. 254–256, 262, 288–299, 308–311. The fullest and most technical discussion of the literature is in K. Koffka, *Principles of Gestalt Psychology* (New York: Harcourt Brace, 1935), pp. 211–264.

SOURCE: E. G. Boring, "The Perception of Objects," *American Journal of Physics,* March–April 1946, 14, 2, 99–107. Reprinted by permission of the American Institute of Physics and E. G. Boring.

image of him on your retinas has doubled. The perception itself, however, changes very little. Or you are at a reception, standing at the end of a large hall. Are the people at the far end dwarfs, only half as tall as the people in the middle of the hall, only a tenth or a twentieth as tall as the man with whom you are talking? Do people change in size at the rate at which the images of them on your retinas change?

What happens is that, under certain circumstances, the brain corrects the perception that depends initially upon the size of the retinal image, corrects it in accordance with other sensory data that indicate the distance from which the retinal image is projected. And the brain can do an excellent job in this kind of correction. At great distances, however, the corrective mechanism becomes inadequate. A man a mile away actually does look small, in part because a mile cannot be perceived accurately. On the other hand, there is doubtless some cerebral correction for the size of a man a mile away, for even the moon—239,000 miles away—shows a tiny correction for the smallness of its retinal image caused by its great distance.

This same tendency to preserve objective constancy happens with visually perceived *shape*. As I stand to one side and look at the top of a circular table, it does not appear as the narrow ellipse that its retinal image is, that the artist would sketch in his projection of the scene. Although every room is full of rectangles, they are perceived not as various diamonds and distorted rectangles, but approximately in their true proportions. The brain corrects the perception for the angle of projection.

So it goes with *brightnesses*. Coal looks black and white paper looks white, provided you know that you are seeing coal and white paper. The white paper may be in shadow and the coal in bright illumination, illumination so bright that the coal reflects more light than the paper. Still the coal looks black and the paper white. The brain takes account of the nature of the objects and corrects the initial impressions that are based solely on illumination.

Sir Isaac Newton observed this phenomenon. He was put to it to prove that gray is a darkish white, because gray things persist in looking gray and white things white. So he rubbed a gray powder on the floor of his chamber in the sunlight and laid nearby in the shadow a piece of white paper. Then he viewed the two objects from a distance so great that their character as objects could not be recognized and saw that the gray powder in sunlight was as white as or whiter than the white paper in shadow. A friend, pressed into service as an observer and asked to judge the patches of brightness before he knew what the objects were, corroborated him.[2]

The general rule also holds for *hue*. If you have the means of knowing from other immediately present sensory data or from past experience what color an object ought to be, then you are apt to see it in its correct color whatever the hue of the illumination. Familiar dresses and upholstery may keep their daylight hues in yellowish artificial illumination, but a new observer with no familiarity to guide him will see them with the yellows favored and the blues diminished. Twenty years ago the technicolor motion pictures were using only two component hues to make colors that should have been trichromatic. One color was put on each side of the film, and the film had only two sides. It was the blues that were cheated. The colors used were a slightly bluish red and a slightly bluish green, which will mix to give good reds and greens, poor yellows and very poor blues. What did the audiences, unused in those days to colored movies, say? That the American flag was beautiful, that the (bluish-green) skies were lovely. But the heroine never wore a pure blue dress (whatever she had on in the studio) because dresses, unlike the sky or the flag's field, can be any color and obey the laws of color mixture without this kind of cerebral mediation. Yet Little Boy [Greenish] Blue in the old-fashioned technicolor might have looked as blue as the sky.

REDUCTION AND REGRESSION

For descriptive purposes it is convenient to say that the sensory data that contribute to a perception can be divided into a core and its context. The *core* is the basic sensory excitation that identifies the perception, that connects it most directly with the object of which it is a perception. The *context* consists of all the other sensory data that modify or correct the data of the core as it forms

[2] I. Newton, *Opticks* (1704; reprint, Bell, 1931), Bk. I, Pt. II, prop. v, exp. 15.

the perception. The context also includes certain acquired properties of the brain, properties that are specific to the particular perception and contribute to the modification of its core. In other words, the context includes knowledge about the perceived object as determined by past experience, that is, by all the brain habits which affect perceiving.[3]

In visual perception the core is the retinal excitation, that is to say, the total optical pattern, specified with respect to the wavelengths and energies involved and the spatial distribution and temporal changes of each. Thus in the visual perception of size with distance variant, the core is the size of the retinal image. The context includes all the clues to the distance of the perceived object—clues of binocular parallax and convergence, and of lenticular accommodation and perspective, as well as the other monocular clues to the awareness of distance. If an observer has before him one disk 10 feet away and another 20 feet away, and undertakes to alter the size of one until it looks the same size as the other, he is likely to come out with two disks of the same physical size. He is obviously not then equating retinal images, for the image of the farther disk has a diameter only half that of the image of the nearer. His brain is using his awareness of distance to make the perception derived from the smaller retinal image look as large as the perception from the larger retinal image. (Whether this correction is an inference, a physiological process or both is a matter that we must consider presently.)

If the perceived object is not a disk, which is unprejudiced as to size, but a man, whose height is, of course, likely to lie between 5 and 7 feet, then this special knowledge is added to the context. Such contextual knowledge does not, however, necessarily prevail. If the visual afterimage of a 6-foot man who is 20 feet away is projected on a wall 60 feet away, the man in the afterimage will be a giant, not far from 18 feet tall—provided the observer is able to perceive the distance to the wall.

These facts of perception can be demonstrated by the *reduction*

[3] This convenient distinction between core and context derives from the one first made by E. B. Titchener, *Textbook of Psychology* (New York: Macmillan, 1910), pp. 367–371; *A Beginner's Psychology* (New York: Macmillan, 1915), pp. 114–121.

of context. When distance is fully apprehended, the perceived size of an object is likely to remain about constant, even though the distance changes greatly and the size of the retinal image changes with it. On the other hand, if you reduce the clues from which distance can be gaged, then you will find that perceived size changes with distance, getting smaller at greater distances. When this reduction of context is partial, the shrinkage of the perception with increasing distance will be less than the shrinkage of the corresponding retinal image. If the reduction could be made complete, if all clues to distance other than the changing size of the retinal image were eliminated, then presumably perceived size would be determined by the only clue remaining, the size of the retinal image. Perceived size and retinal size would then always keep the same proportional relation. With a receding object perceived size would shrink as fast as the retinal image, for the observer would be wholly unaware of the recession, unless he used his awareness of diminishing size as a clue to the perception of the distance. He might.

Some writers have preferred to think of the converse of this relationship. Reduction of context reduces perception to its bare core, but increase of context increases correspondence of the perception to the real object. If you know how far away a seen object is, you may be able to perceive its true size. If you know that that gray is coal, it may look black. This effect of context to make the perception resemble the permanent object that is being perceived rather than the perceptual core has been called by Thouless *regression toward the real object*.[4] Regression toward the object is the opposite of reduction toward the core. Regression toward the object occurs with increase of context. Reduction toward the core is secured by decrease of context.

It was Katz who in 1911 first applied this term *reduction*, not to the case of size and distance, but to color and illumination.[5] Take the illuminated coal and the shaded white paper. The coal looks black, the paper white, although the coal reflects more light. But now interpose what Katz called a *reduction screen*, a screen with

[4] R. H. Thouless, "Phenomenal Regression to the Real Object," *British Journal of Psychology* 1931, **21**, 339–359; 1931, **22**, 1–30.

[5] D. Katz, "Die Erscheinungsweisen der Farben und ihre Beeinflussung durch die individuelle Erfahrung," *Z. Psychologie*, Suppl. **7**, 1911, esp. 36–39.

two small circular openings in it. Through one opening you see a patch of the surface of the coal, through the other a patch of the surface of the paper. You do not see enough to identify either object, and at once the patch that is the coal appears as a gray lighter than the patch that is the white paper. By the use of the screen you have reduced the context that identifies the objects, reduced it to the core of this perception, the total illumination.

PERCEIVED SIZE AND DISTANCE: HISTORY

Most persons think that the perceived size of an object varies proportionately with retinal size of its image and thus with the visual angle subtended by the object. There seem to be two reasons for this belief.

(1) To assume that visual size is measured by visual angle brings perception into the geometry of optics in a simple and logical way. Euclid in his *Optica* worked in terms of this optical geometry, equating visual angle to perceived size; yet even he noted that the magnitude of the perception does not always accord with the perceived size. Still Euclid provided the simple rule that has ever since been quite generally accepted. The principle that perceived size varies with the visual angle subtended and thus with the size of the retinal image we shall call *Euclid's rule*.

(2) Progress in understanding visual perception during the last three centuries has consisted primarily in finding out how the eye works. From the ancient belief that objects give off tiny images of themselves, images which are conducted by the optic nerve to the sensorium for perception, we have come to an understanding of optical projection upon the retina. In general, nineteenth-century physiology held that the brain perceives not the object itself but its projection on the retina and the consequent excitation of the optic nerve. (Why else should there have been a problem as to why we see right side up when the retinal image is upside down?) When perception was found not to correspond exactly with the stimulus object, one looked—all through the nineteenth century—to the eye for the explanation of the illusion, for but little was known about the supraretinal physiology of vision.

Nevertheless, there have been constant reminders that visual angle (retinal size) and perceived size do not always correspond. There were the eighteenth-century philosophers who tried to figure out the curve along which trees, bordering on an avenue, should be planted in order that the two lines of trees might look parallel and everywhere equidistant, when viewed from a specified end. And there were the psychologists in the period 1889–1913 who determined these curves experimentally. Various scientists remarked in the middle nineteenth century that Euclid's rule does not hold. If you view a length l at a distance d and compare it with a length $2l$ at a distance $2d$, then l and $2l$ form retinal images of the same size and should, by Euclid's rule, appear to be the same size. Actually, it is easily noted that $2l$ looks longer than l; yet that observation seldom excites curiosity since, it can be said, if $2l$ really is longer than l, why should it not look longer? Euclid gave a reason why it should not, but plainly he was wrong.

Then there was Emmert's law in 1881, the law that the perceived linear size of an afterimage is proportional to the distance of the background on which the image is projected. Emmert's law contradicts Euclid's. In an afterimage the size of the retinal image is fixed; how then does the size of the perception alter so greatly? Yet the fact is that the afterimage of a near object projected on a far background looks gigantic when retinal size does not change at all.

In the present century there has arisen in connection with the tenets of Gestalt psychology the conception of *size constancy*, the hypothesis that the perceived size of an object remains constant irrespective of the distance at which the object is perceived. There has been a great deal of misunderstanding and controversy about this matter; but that need not concern us, for the facts are plain.[6]

PERCEIVED SIZE AND DISTANCE: MEASUREMENT

Let me now summarize an experiment that Holway and I completed a few years ago, an experiment that measures the dependence of perceived size upon distance, and that also shows how the

[6] For the history of research and observation, see Boring, reference 1 (1942), pp. 288–299, 308–311.

resulting functions depend upon the context and how the effective context can be analyzed by successively reducing it.[7]

We seated the observer at the right-angled junction of two halls, facing the convex corner at 45° from the longitudinal axes of the halls. By turning his head from side to side he could look down one hall or the other, alternating at will. We worked at night in complete darkness except for the light that came from the two illuminated stimulus disks.

The standard stimulus was a disk of light, projected from a lantern on a translucent screen. It was placed in the hall at the right at distances from the observer varying from 10 to 120 feet. The size of the disk was made proportional to the distance so that it always subtended at the observer an angle of 1°. It was the perceived size of this disk at different distances that was the subject of investigation.

In the hall at the left was a comparison stimulus for measuring perceived size. It consisted of a projected disk of light which remained always at 10 feet from the observer. Its size could be changed by the use of a long series of apertures with which the projection lantern was provided. The observer varied the size of this comparison stimulus until he was satisfied that he had made it the same perceived size as the standard stimulus. This judgment is not always easy when the disks are at different distances, but the difficulty arises only in the final adjustments of the comparison stimulus. Great differences in perceived size at great differences in distance are easily observed with immediate certainty, even when the judgment departs widely from Euclid's rule of the visual angle.

The results of this procedure are plotted in Figure 1. The two dashed lines, *B* and *F*, represent theoretical relationships.

The function B is for perceived size constant, irrespective of distance. The reason this line rises (slope $= \tan 1°$) is that we increased the size of the standard stimulus in proportion to its distance, keeping its angular subtension constant at 1°. We did this in order to avoid any physiological distortion that might arise from

---

[7] A. H. Holway and E. G. Boring, "Determinants of Apparent Visual Size with Distance Variant," *American Journal of Psychology*, 1941, 54, 21–37.

exciting different sizes of retinal areas. The straight line *B* is thus the function for perceived *size constancy* because it is the function for a comparison stimulus increasing with the standard stimulus and remaining equal to it, when the standard stimulus is increased with distance in order to keep angular subtension constant.

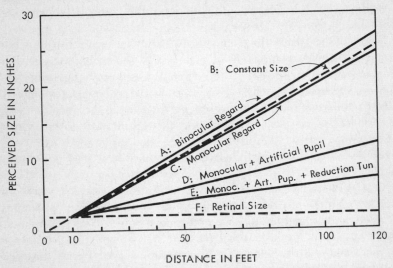

FIGURE 1. Visually perceived size as a function of the distance of the perceived object. The perceived standard disk at every distance is of such physical size that its diameter subtends an angle of 1° to the observer. Its perceived size (ordinate scale) is the diameter, in inches, of a comparison disk 10 feet from the observer and equated in perceived size to the standard disk. The six functions shown are as follows: *A*, free binocular regard; the perceived size increased slightly with distance; *B*, constant size, the function for no change of perceived size with distance; *C*, monocular regard; the perceived size diminished slightly with distance; *D*, monocular regard with use of artificial pupil; great decrease of perceived size with distance; *E*, monocular regard, with use of artificial pupil and reduction tunnel; still greater decrease in perceived size; *F*, retinal size, the function for decrease in perceived size proportional to the actual size of the retinal image (visual angle subtended).

The horizontal line F is the function for proportionality of perceived size to retinal size (visual angle). It represents *Euclid's rule*. Since the visual angle was kept constant at 1°, proportionality of perceived size to visual angle would in this case be constant.

The other four functions show what happens with reduction.

Although the observed points are not shown here, the fits to straight lines are close.

Free binocular regard is shown in function *A*. If size constancy were to be the rule, we should expect *A* to coincide with *B*. To our surprise it lay slightly above *B*, for the four more reliable of the five observers. A receding object tends (under these conditions) to get a little larger in perception while its retinal image is becoming very much smaller. Perceived size, in other words, is not only constant; it is "more than constant!" The position of this function suggests that the binocular mechanism is set to compensate immediately for shrinkage of the retinal image by increasing distance and that under these conditions it overcompensates slightly. That finding might be an argument for the phenomenon's being the consequence of a property of the brain and not a matter of inference. It is doubtful, however, that any good can come from trying to distinguish between inference and its brain physiology.

Our first step was to reduce binocular to monocular vision by putting a patch over one of the observer's eyes. Function *C* resulted, a close approximation to size constancy. Some of the individual functions for *C* lay just above *B*, some below, and the average, as shown, was a little below. Later experiments by Taylor and myself with two men, each of whom had lost the use of one eye more than ten years earlier, gave functions similar to those on which *C* in Figure 1 is based.[8] For this reason we assumed that monocular vision, either temporary or permanent, follows closely the law of size constancy, and that overcompensation may sometimes result when the use of a second eye is added.

The next reduction of the distance context was to add to monocular observation an artificial pupil, which eliminated accommodation of the iris diaphragm and reduced the effectiveness of the lenticular accommodation by stopping the lens down to 1.8 mm. With this situation there were more individual differences among observers, but the reliability of each observer remained high. Function *D* in Figure 1 is the average result. It shows that reduction

[8] D. W. Taylor and E. G. Boring, "Apparent Size as a Function of Distance for Monocular Observers," *American Journal of Psychology*, 1942, **55**, 102–105.

toward the proportionality to retinal size (Euclid's rule, function F) has progressed greatly.

The use of monocular vision with an artificial pupil still left some visible clues to the distance of the stimulus. The faint light from the two stimuli showed vaguely to the dark-adapted eye the perspective of the walls, floor and ceiling of the corridor. To get rid of these clues we constructed a "reduction tunnel" of heavy black cloth, 3 feet square in cross section and capable of being extended to 100 feet long. The observer viewed the standard stimulus through it, and a further reduction resulted, as shown by function E in Figure 1.

Complete reduction should give an observed function that coincides with F. We were unable to obtain it. Not with all this effort and artifice could we make Euclid's commonly accepted law of perceived size as proportional to visual angle come true! Yet the function F must be found if all clues to distance are eliminated. The results plotted in E show the observers discriminating different distances fairly accurately. If the function E were known, then the distance could be told from a knowledge of the equations of perceived size. The failure to reduce to F means that there are still clues to distance left.

Figure 1 is confusing because the standard stimulus was kept constant in angular size instead of in linear size. Figure 2 is simpler, showing how the size of a constant disk would appear to change if it approached the observer or receded from him. The contractions and expansions are shown as ratios to the linear size of the disk at 10 feet away from the observer. Figure 2 is derived from Figure 1 by making the assumption that the relationships of Figure 1 would hold for areas of the retina differing considerably from 1°, and the further assumption that difference in perceived size is proportional to the amount of change necessary in the stimulus to abolish difference in perceived size. This last statement means, for example, that if two disks at different distances looked the same size and one had a diameter four times the diameter of the other, then, if the diameters were made actually equal, one of them would appear to be one-quarter the length of the other. It is a plausible assumption, but not necessarily correct. The functions of Figure 2 yield curves because they are reciprocal to linear functions.

In view of these consistent results there cannot be much doubt that perceived size depends upon more than the size of the retinal image, that the clue from the retinal image is corrected by those contexts that establish the distance of the perceived object, and that the correction can be fully adequate when the context is not

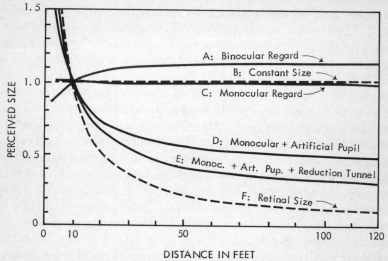

FIGURE 2.   Visually perceived size as a function of the distance of the perceived object. These curves are derived from those of Figure 1 by the use of certain simple assumptions. Perceived size is shown as ratios to the perceived size of the stimulus object at a distance of 10 feet and subtending an angle of 1°. See legend to Figure 1 for further specification of the six functions shown.

too greatly reduced. Monocular vision in the near-dark is good enough to keep size constant. Binocular vision in the near-dark may do too good a job. We have no measurements to show what happens with the perspective clues that good illumination in a furnished hall would produce.

These functions hold up to a distance of 120 feet, and possibly up to 200 feet. What happens at great distances? We have only casual observation and one experiment to show. A man a mile away looks small, even though seen with two eyes in broad daylight over a terrain that furnishes excellent perspective clues. Is he reduced as much in perceived size as is his image on my retina?

We do not know. The experiments on great distances have yet to be made, and should be made.

There is, however, one experiment on the perceived size of a distant object—the moon. The moon's disk subtends about ½°, but the horizon moon may be matched to a comparison stimulus that is 12 feet away and that subtends an angle of 3°, and a moon in elevation to a comparison stimulus of 2°.[9] In other words, a disk, 2,160 miles in diameter and 239,000 miles away, appears the same size as a disk 7½ inches in diameter 12 feet away. If Euclid's law held, the moon would match in size a disk 1¼ inches in diameter at 12 feet distance, because this little disk and the moon would each subtend an angle of ½°. There is for the moon no size constancy. The real moon does not look so big as a 239,000-mile disk 12 feet away! The lack of distance contexts for the moon nearly reduces its perception to the law of retinal size, yet not quite. The perceived dummy moon 12 feet away regresses toward the real object to an amount six times what its retinal size would justify, although it is still only one 18-millionth of the size of the real moon. It seems that the great but nearly indeterminate distance of the moon provides just enough context to shift the perceptual size a little bit away from what retinal size alone would give, shifting it in the direction of size constancy, in the direction of regression toward the real object.

LOGIC OR PHYSIOLOGY?

It is an interesting question as to just what is going on when an organism uses the totality of available relevant clues or cues in modeling a perception so that it resembles as nearly as possible the permanent object which is being perceived. From one point of view, the conscious organism seems to be using *clues* to form an inference as to the real nature of the object which is revealed to it through various sense data. From another point of view, the organism seems to be using the various sensory excitations as *cues* to bring a given perception onto the stage of consciousness in

[9] E. G. Boring, "The Moon Illusion," *American Journal of Physics*, 1943, 11, 55–60, and references there cited.

accordance with a script in which the stage directions are the integrative properties of the brain. *Clues* and *cues*—both words are used, and they represent two theories of perception, which are often opposed to each other without their being truly incompatible.

Helmholtz recognized this dilemma when, in 1866, he undertook to explain these perceptual phenomena by an appeal to the concept of *unconscious inference* (*unbewusster Schluss*).[10] The perception is essentially, he said, a conclusion formed from evidence by inductive inference. The process of its formation, while like a conscious inference, is actually unconscious. It is normally irresistible and instantaneous, although, Helmholtz thought, it can be unlearned and was therefore probably learned in the first place.

On that last matter Helmholtz certainly made too large a generalization. That coal is black is doubtless learned, and perhaps an artist might unlearn coal's color enough to see it in sunlight as light gray. That is not certain, though. It is possible that the artist sees his light-gray paint as black when he realizes it is coal. Some of the optical illusions break down or diminish under critical inspection, but others persist as inevitably compulsory. No amount of inspection, thought or knowledge will teach you to see the circles of Figure 3 as anything other than spirals. They are circles though —perfect circles. That they are closed figures appears at once if you start at *a* and follow the circle around until you come back to *a* again.

An illusion is, however, not a good example of unconscious inference, for it involves faulty logic or physiologic, whichever it is. It does not produce a perception that is faithful to its true object. A much better instance of compulsory unconscious inference is the stereoscopic perception of depth.

In stereoscopic vision the evidence for depth or solidity lies in that slight disparity of the two retinal images which is furnished by binocular parallax. Given a few constants of the binocular system, the forms and sizes of the two disparate images, and the assign-

[10] H. Helmholtz, *Physiological Optics* (1866, tr., New York: Optical Society of America, 1925), Vol. III, pp. 1–35; *Die Thatsachen in der Wahrnehmung* (Hirschwald, 1879). Helmholtz seems to have had the idea of unconscious inference as early as 1855. See E. G. Boring, *A History of Experimental Psychology* (New York: Appleton-Century, 1929), pp. 300–304.

ment of one image to the left eye and the other to the right, and you can figure out geometrically by conscious inference what the dimensions in depth are. The visual mechanism, however, makes this inference instantaneously and unconsciously. If the stereograms are photographs, rich in detail, it is as impossible ever to see the disparity between them, as it is to be aware of disparity in the binocular observation of a solid object. Only in very simple stereoscopic images, such as the outline drawings of geometric

FIGURE 3. Twisted cord illusion. The perceived spirals are actually perfect circles, as can be found by starting at *a* and following the apparent spiral back to *a* again. [Adapted from J. Fraser, *British Journal of Psychology*, 1908, **2**, 307–320.]

figures, does one sometimes see the disparity as doubled lines first, before the doubling disappears and the images pull together into a single solid figure. In the perception the brain reaches a correct inferential conclusion as to the depth of the perceived object, but the process is no more conscious than is the inference of an electronic computer which calculates almost instantly from relevant data a range and elevation and correctly aims a gun.

It is in fact this electric analogy that answers quite well the question as to whether the integrative process in perceiving is logical or physiological. It is both. There is no contradiction. The inference is as logical and as unconscious as it is when made electrically in a machine.

The Gestalt psychologists—Wertheimer, Köhler and Koffka—have emphasized the notion that perceptual integration in the brain is due to the operation of certain dynamic patterns of "force" that often correct or alter the perceptual form in ways that resemble closely the operation of mechanical or electric field forces.[11] Frequently this process results in what might be called a simplification.

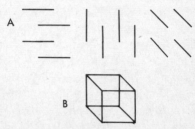

FIGURE 4.   Dynamics of the visual field. The 12 lines of A, three sets of four lines each, all seen as lying in the plane of the paper, when superposed to make B, form a perceived solid in which the 12 lines no longer appear to lie on the plane of the paper.

Two disparate images, one on each retina, constitute a confusion and make no sense. Put them together and you have both simplicity and sense—a single tridimensional object. Helmholtz would have called that unconscious inference, but the Gestalt psychologists eschew *inference* in favor of *field forces*.

Figure 4 is similar to a figure of Koffka's. Above, at A, you see three sets of four lines each. At B you see the three sets superposed, and the 12 lines arranged in this relation give you the perception

[11] The leaders of the movement called Gestalt psychology are Max Wertheimer (1880–1943), Kurt Koffka (1886–1941) and Wolfgang Köhler (1887–). The movement began in Germany with experiments on perception and with the development of a theory of perception. See reference 1 for Koffka's discussion and the books that give other references to this large literature. A very important contribution is W. Köhler, *Die physischen Gestalten in Ruhe und im stationären Zustand* (Vieweg, 1920); see also his *The Place of Value in a World of Facts* (New York: Liveright, 1938), *Dynamics in Psychology* (New York: Liveright, 1940), and Köhler and H. Wallach, "Figural After-effects," *Proceedings of the American Philosophical Society*, 1944, 88, 269–357.

of depth. It is practicably impossible to see them any more as lying flat in the plane of the paper, as they did in A. The cube of B insists on appearing solid, although it is reversible and may be seen in either of two perspectives. Is the cube simpler than the 12 lines? Well, there is only one cube, and perhaps one is simpler than 12. At any rate the cube is more sensible than the 12 lines because it is an object. The brain has here integrated an object. For binocular parallax it redintegrates an object.

There is, then, no objection to be raised to the idea that brain properties should operate to establish the conclusions to inferences. Physical properties do in the electric computer. They might in the brain. It takes a brain to do any conscious inferring, and the brain operates always under natural physical law. There is no real contradiction between Helmholtz and the Gestalt psychologists.

It is, moreover, clear that these integrative properties of the brain are both native and acquired, dependent upon both *heredity* and *learning*. The dynamics of stereoscopy and of the perceptions of Figures 3 and 4 seem almost certainly native neural properties and not acquired. Seeing objects in their true colors and brightnesses, irrespective of the illumination, must be learned. The chromosomes take no account of what colors are in the American flag. It would be a bold man who would assert at present that constancy of perceived shape is either wholly learned or wholly native. We do not know. What then about the correction of retinal size for distance?

There are experiments which show that chickens can learn to choose larger grains of corn and reject smaller, when the difference in size is of the order of only 10 percent. When they have acquired this discrimination, then they will choose remote large grains in preference to small grains nearby, although the retinal images of the remote large grains may be only one fifth the size of the retinal images of the near small grains.[12] Still the chickens may have learned to take distance into account.

Children do not do so well as adults, nor young children so well as older, in matching boxes for actual size when the boxes lie on

[12] W. Köhler, "Optische Untersuchungen am Schimpansen und am Haushuhn," *Abhandl. preuss. Akad. Wiss., Phys.-math. Klasse*, No. 3, 18–139 (1915); W. Götz, "Experimentelle Untersuchungen zum Problem der Sehgrössenkonstanz beim Haushuhn," Z. *Psychologie*, 1926, 99, 247–260.

the floor at different distances away.[13] There are individual differences among adults, and anything that tends to distort the perception of distance seems to affect the perception of size, whereas the best judgments of objective size are got from the observers who can estimate the distances most correctly.[14] Such findings suggest that learning plays a role.

On the other hand, it is somewhat implausible that, in learning to compensate for changing size of the retinal image with changing distance, one should acquire a habit for overcompensation (function A in Figures 1 and 2). Overcompensation seems to imply the operation of more basic mechanisms than those that are learned. Still there is no conclusive evidence. One might acquire separately by learning a number of corrective processes which, all working concurrently, would then overshoot the mark. If that conclusion is correct, we are still left with the problem as to why the organism would learn to compensate just a little bit for the small size of the moon's image on the retina. If that correction is learned, it must have been carried over from some other experience.

Actually the decision on this question does not matter. No inherited function is ever quite unaffected by learning, and no learned function is ever able to operate entirely without dependence on what is given it by inheritance. If the perception of size with distance variant depends on both chromosomes and practice, it will be like almost every other psychophysiological function.

BIOLOGICAL USE OF PERCEPTION

The physiology of perception is uncertain, but its biology is clear. The function of perception is to transform chaotic sense experience into the relative stability of permanent objects, the objects which

[13] F. Beyrl, "Über die Grössenauffassung bei Kindern," Z. *Psychologie*, 1926, **100**, 344–371; H. Frank, "Die Sehgrössenkonstanz bei Kindern," *Psychologische Forschung*, 1928, **10**, 102–106.

[14] R. H. Thouless, "Individual Differences in Phenomenal Regression," *British Journal of Psychology*, 1932, **22**, 216–241; M. R. Sheehan, "A Study of Individual Consistency in Phenomenal Constancy," *Archives of Psychology*, 1938, No. 222; B. E. Holaday, "Die Grössenkonstanz der Sehdinge bei Variation der inneren und äusseren Wahrnehmungsbedingungen," *Arch. ges. Psychol.*, 1933, **88**, 419–486.

cause the experience or are implied by the experience, whichever way you like to look at it. An object can be regarded as an as-if theory of experience. Experience would be as it is if there were permanent objects. And the properties of the objects thus become generalizations about experience. So perception, in getting back of experience to the objects, is performing even in primitive man and the animals the same function that science performs in man's civilization. As the purpose of scientific theories is economy of thought, so the purpose of perception is economy of thinking. It picks out and establishes what is permanent and therefore important to the organism for its survival and welfare.

To see a gray as coal is useful. It is to know that this gray will burn and give heat. To see a verdigris as blue is to recognize your country's flag. To see a diamond as square is to recognize the book or the table for what it is, which is important, and to ignore the effect of your own angular relation to it, which, since it changes as you move, is unimportant. To see a distant object with a small retinal image as large and a near object with a large retinal image as small is to get away from the unimportant retinal images to the great importance of the sizes of objects. A chicken by that means gets all the big grains of corn, no matter how far away they are. Perhaps the greatest perceptual achievement of the organism is the way in which it receives on bidimensional retinas optical projections of the tridimensional world, losing, it would seem, all the tridimensionality, and then, taking immediate physiological account of the disparity of binocular parallax and other clues when they are available, instantaneously puts the solid object together again in perception, recovering the tridimensionality of the real object which had seemed irrevocably lost.

[2]

Apparent Visual Size as a Function of Distance for Children and Adults

H. PHILIP ZEIGLER and H. W. LEIBOWITZ

There is some question in the literature as to whether size-constancy varies with age.[1] Data are, however, lacking from an investigation of size-constancy for which a wide range of distances is available and for which a functional relationship can be plotted. The present study was designed to obtain such results.

APPARATUS AND PROCEDURE

The procedure was modeled after that used by Holway and Boring.[2] A series of standard stimulus-objects, made from 1-inch diameter wooden dowels, were prepared such that at the distances used in the study, the objects subtended a visual angle of 0.96° at S's eye. The comparison-object, also a 1-inch diameter dowel, was so arranged that the visible portion of its length could be continuously varied by moving it up or down through a hole cut in the center of a board. The remainder of the comparison-object was hidden from S by a suitably placed curtain. S was seated at a distance of 5 feet from the comparison-object, which was approxi-

[1] Franz Beyrl, "Ueber die Grössenauffassung bei Kindern," Z. Psychologie, 1926, **100**, 344–371; H. Frank, "Untersuchung über Sehgrössenkonstanz bei Kindern," Psychologische Forschung, 1926, **7**, 137–145; "Die Sehgrössenkonstanz bei Kindern," ibid., 1928, **10**, 102–106; Wilhelm Burzlaff, "Methodologische Beiträge zum Problem der Farbenkonstanz," Z. Psychologie, 1931, **119**, 177–235.

[2] A. H. Holway and E. G. Boring, "Determinants of Apparent Visual Size with Distance Variant," The American Journal of Psychology, 1941, **54**, 21–37.

SOURCE: H. P. Zeigler and H. W. Leibowitz, "Apparent Visual Size as a Function of Distance for Children and Adults," The American Journal of Psychology, March 1957, **70**, 1, 106–109. Reprinted by permission of The American Journal of Psychology.

mately at eye-level. The standard objects were fitted into small black wooden blocks and mounted on a black metal stand 3 feet from the floor in front of and slightly to one side of the comparison-object.

The experiment was conducted in a room 108 x 22 feet. From *S's* position three windows were visible on one side of the room and one at the extreme end. There were several pieces of furniture visible along the walls. Illumination was provided by six 100-w. bulbs in addition to the windows, and the experiments were conducted in the early afternoon and only on sunny days.

Five distances were used; 10, 30, 60, 80, and 100 feet. For each distance *S* made four judgments, two ascending and two descending. (The actual manipulation of the comparison stimulus was done by *E* at *S's* direction.) The distances were presented in a random order and, between successive trials with new distances, *S* was so blindfolded that he could not see *E* setting up the standard objects.

The instructions for both children and adults were as follows.

I am going to move this stick (pointing to the comparison-object) up and down. I want you to tell me when it looks as high as the one out there (pointing to the standard object).

S was told to disregard the stand or the wooden block and to base his judgments on the height of the standards. *E* avoided giving any information as to whether the standards were of the same or different sizes. *S* was also instructed to make all judgments with binocular regard and to wear glasses if needed.

The *Ss* were 13 in number (8 boys, ranging from 7 to 9 years of age, and 5 men, from 18 to 24 years of age) all resident at a summer camp. The men were told they were to serve as controls for the experiment with the children. For the boys, the experiment was part of a "scouting" game which included outdoor as well as indoor estimates of the sizes of various objects.

RESULTS

The results for the children are given in Table 1 and for the adults in Table 2. Both sets of data are plotted in Figure 1. On this

TABLE 1

Matched Size (in Inches) of Standard Stimulus-Object as a Function
of Distance (Children)

Distance of Standard (in Feet)

S	Age (in Yr.)	10	30	60	80	100
				Size of Test Object (in Inches)		
		2	6	12	16	20
1	9	1.3	3.3	2.9	3.5	3.3
2	8	1.9	4.3	7.8	8.2	9.2
3	8	1.5	3.1	5.3	6.4	5.5
4	7	2.9	4.1	6.6	7.8	9.4
5	8	3.1	5.1	9.9	11.1	13.1
6	8	2.5	5.2	8.3	8.0	8.3
7	8	2.1	4.8	11.1	8.2	10.9
8	9	.8	1.1	1.4	1.2	1.1
Mean		2.0	3.9	6.7	6.8	7.6
SD		.8	1.3	3.3	3.6	4.0
Brunswik ratio		1.00	.58	.52	.39	.35

TABLE 2

Matched Size (in Inches) of Standard Stimulus-Object as a Function
of Distance (Adults)

Distance of Standard (in Feet)

S	Age (in Yr.)	10	30	60	80	100
				Size of Test Object (in Inches)		
		2	6	12	16	20
1	20	2.2	6.4	8.9	15.1	15.7
2	24	2.6	6.2	7.9	9.8	15.0
3	18	2.4	5.9	10.4	11.6	12.3
4	20	2.3	5.6	13.6	18.8	21.1
5	19	2.9	7.4	12.4	17.8	22.6
Mean		2.5	6.3	10.6	14.6	17.3
SD		.36	.78	2.3	3.8	4.3
Brunswik ratio		1.50	1.06	.87	.91	.86

plot a horizontal line represents the law of the visual angle; a theoretical condition in which perceived size can be predicted on the basis of geometrical optics. The law of size-constancy is represented by a line of slope 0.017 (tan 0.96°). If perceived size were independent of distance, that is, perfect size-constancy, the data would fall along this theoretical function.

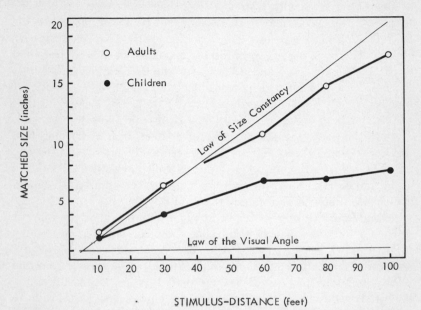

STIMULUS–DISTANCE (feet)

FIGURE 1.   Mean matched size as a function of stimulus-distance for a group of adults and of children. The size of the test-object was adjusted so as always to subtend a constant visual angle.

It can be seen from Figure 1 that the data for the adults fall very close to the prediction in terms of size-constancy as previously reported by Holway and Boring. The data for the children however, fall at positions on the matched size-axis closer to the line representing the law of the visual angle. Differences between the means of matched sizes for adults and children were calculated for all distances above 10 feet. A Mann-Whitney non-parametric u-test indicates that these differences are significant ($u < 0.01$ for 30, 80, 100 ft.; $u < 0.05$ for 60 ft.).

DISCUSSION

The results of the present investigation demonstrate closer agreement with the law of size-constancy for a group of adults than for a group of children. Such results are consistent with the conclusions of Beyrl, but differ with respect to the magnitude of the difference in size-constancy.[3] As has been pointed out by Frank, all of Beyrl's Ss, including his 2-year-old children, demonstrate rather high constancy.[4] Brunswik ratios computed for his data, which were obtained at distances between 6 and 37 feet, for the 2-year-old group range from 0.77 to 0.92 for a disk test-object, and from 0.87 to 0.95 for blocks. For his 8-year-old group (n = 2) the ratios vary from 0.97 to 0.99 for both kinds of test-objects. Brunswik ratios for the children in the present study are 1.00 at 10 feet, 0.58 at 30 feet, and drop to 0.35 at 100 feet. Thus, the present study agrees with Beyrl's conclusion that size-constancy is not as well developed in children as in adults, but differs in that for comparable stimulus-distances the children show less constancy than did Beyrl's.

In addition, the present experiment, utilizing a greater range of distances, indicates that the differences between children and adults increases with the distance of the test-object. This can be clearly seen from the shape of the curve in Figure 1. The function for the adults is nearly linear, and lies close to the line representing the law of size-constancy. The curve for the children rises less rapidly with distance and approaches a limiting value at about 60 feet. The differences between the mean matched size at 60 and 100 feet are not significant for the children ($p > 0.05$) and are significant for the adults ($p < 0.01$).

With respect to inter-S variability, the present results are consistent with those of previous investigators. As has been pointed out by Smith, studies of size-constancy typically demonstrate an increase in variability with distance.[5] That this also holds true for the

[3] Franz Beyrl, "Ueber die Grössenauffassung bei Kindern," *Z. Psychologie*, 1926, **100**, 369.

[4] H. Frank, "Untersuchung über Sehgrössenkonstanz bei Kindern," *Psychologische Forschung*, 1926, **7**, 103.

[5] W. M. Smith, A Methodological Study of Size-Distance Perception," *Journal of Psychology*, 1953, **35**, 143–153.

present investigation is evident from inspection of the standard deviations in Tables 1 and 2.

The present results, obtained over a range of 90 feet, demonstrates that the functional relationship between matched size and distance is different for adults and children. Such results are interpreted as supporting the view that size-constancy increases with age.

SUMMARY

The function relating matched size to distance was determined for groups of children and adults. The Ss matched a comparison-object to one of a series of standard objects located at various distances but so adjusted in size as always to subtend a constant visual angle. The results for the adults lie close to the theoretical line representing the law of size-constancy. The results for the children were more in agreement with the law of the visual angle. The adult-curve is nearly a straight line, while that for the children approaches a limiting value at 60 feet. These data are viewed as lending support to the thesis that size-constancy increases as a function of age.

[3]
Adaptation to Disarranged Eye-Hand Coordination in the Distance-Dimension

RICHARD HELD and MELVIN SCHLANK

Although Helmholtz was the first to study adaptation to a sensory-motor disarrangement—reduction of the errors of hand-eye coordination induced by a prism before the eye [1]—Stratton's study of

[1] H. L. F. von Helmholtz, *Handbuch der physiologischen Optik*, 1867, 3, 601–602.

SOURCE: R. Held and M. Schlank, "Adaptation to Disarranged Eye-Hand Coordination in the Distance-Dimension," *The American Journal of Psychology*, December 1959, **72**, 4, 603–605. Reprinted by permission of *The American Journal of Psychology*.

inverted vision is generally considered the classic in this field.[2] Recently Kohler reported the most extensive studies yet performed, revealing new and unexpected kinds of adaptation.[3] Most investigators have concentrated on the development of apparatus to produce the disarrangement and on the measurement of the consequences of exposure to novel conditions, but few have attempted to vary systematically the conditions of exposure to determine which are critical for adaptation. This study is one of a series designed to isolate the critical conditions.[4]

Holst used the terms *re-afference* and *ex-afference* to distinguish between sensory stimulation resulting from self-produced movement and sensory stimulation independent of such movement.[5] The results of two experiments on prolonged exposure to disarranged visual-motor coordination (prisms before the eyes) are consistent with the hypothesis that re-afferent stimulation is necessary for adaptation.[6] In both experiments, re-afferent stimulation produced significant shifts of localization in the adaptive direction, while ex-afferent stimulation did not. The technique of these experiments consisted essentially of equating all conditions of exposure other than the agent producing the bodily movement. Re-afferent visual stimulation was obtained in one experiment when S walked a path while viewing his environment and in the other experiment when S moved his arm before his eyes. Comparable ex-afferent stimulation was obtained when E either moved S while seated in a wheel

[2] G. M. Stratton, "Vision Without Inversion of the Retinal Image," *Psychological Review*, 1897, 4, 341–360, 463–481.

[3] Ivo Kohler, "Ueber Aufbau und Wandlungen der Wahrnehmungenswelt; inbesondere überbedingte Empfindungen," *Sitzungsber. Oest. Akad. Wiss.*, 1951, 227, 1–118.

[4] Richard Held, "Shifts in Binaural Localization After Prolonged Exposures to Atypical Combinations of Stimuli," *The American Journal of Psychology*, 1955, 68, 526–548; Joseph Bossom and Richard Held, "Shifts in Egocentric Localization Following Prolonged Displacement of the Retinal Image," *American Psychologist*, 1957, 12, 454 (Abstract); Richard Held and A. V. Hein, "Adaptation of Disarranged Hand-Eye Coordination Contingent upon Re-afferent Stimulation," *Percept. mot. Skills*, 1958, 8, 87–90.

[5] E. von Holst, "Relations Between the Central Nervous System and the Peripheral Organs, *British Journal of Animal Behaviour*, 1954, 2, 89–94.

[6] Blossom and Held, "Shifts in Egocentric Localization Following Prolonged Displacement of the Retinal Image," *American Psychologist*, 1957, 12, 454; Held and Hein, "Adaptation of Disarranged Hand-Eye Coordination Contingent upon Re-afferent Stimulation," *Percept. mot. Skills*, 1958, 8, 87–90.

chair over the path formerly walked or moved S's arm. Since the changes in optical stimulation under both conditions were very similar, differences in amount of adaptation were attributed to the difference in the agents producing movement.

METHOD

Figure 1 shows S in the apparatus under the two conditions. In Figure 1A, he marks the apparent location of a target to provide a measure of his eye-hand coordination. In Figure 1B, he views a virtual image of his hand at a distance optically greater than normal. The apparatus consisted of an upper and lower lightbox. The

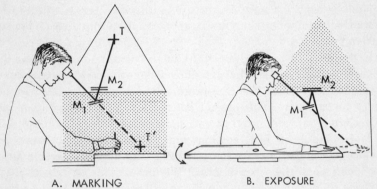

A. MARKING   B. EXPOSURE

FIGURE 1. Schematic representation of S in the apparatus under two experimental conditions.

upper lightbox contained the target, T—three black spots on a white field forming an equilateral triangle 3 in. on a side. S's hand was in the lower lightbox. A half-silvered mirror, M_2, divided the two lightboxes. Whether S viewed T or his hand depended on whether the upper or the lower lightbox was illuminated. The position of a double-throw switch determined which one of the lightboxes was illuminated. A biting-board held S's head in a fixed position throughout each session.

During marking (Figure 1A), when the upper lightbox was illuminated and the lower lightbox darkened, light from T passed through M_2 and was reflected into S's eyes from M_1, a fully reflecting first-surface mirror. S saw the virtual image of T at location T′ which coincided with the marking surface. *He did not see his hand or the marking surface* because his vision was restricted by apertures to the field reflected in M_1. S was instructed to mark successively the apparent location of the three target-points nine times, for a total of 27 marks.

During exposure (Figure 1B), the upper lightbox was blacked-out while the lower lightbox was illuminated. Under these conditions, the half-silvered mirror, M_2, reflected light from the hand to M_1 and then to S's eyes. Looking into M_1, S saw his hand at the increased optical distance. The increase in distance averaged 3 in. at the level of the marking surface. S's hand was strapped to the swivel shown in Figure 1B. Two conditions of exposure were used. The movement of S's arm was caused either by his own efforts (*self-produced movement*) or by E's movement of the swivel (*passive movement*).

Experiments with each of 15 Ss were conducted in two sessions; one with self-produced movement and the other with passive movement. Eight Ss had the self-produced movement first, while the other seven began with passive movement. The two sessions were separated by at least one day.

The schedule of both sessions was as follows. (1) Pre-exposure marking (Figure 1A): With his unseen hand, S marked the apparent locations of the three points of the target. This set of marks gave a measure of S's eye-hand coordination before exposure. (2) Exposure (Figure 1B): S viewed the mirrored image of his hand on the swivel at the optically increased distance as it moved back and forth in a small a.c. (3) Post-exposure marking (Figure 1A): S was instructed to mark the apparent locations of the target-points as he had done in the pre-exposure marking. The difference in positions of the pre- and post-exposure markings measured the influence of the intervening exposure.

In the exposure with self-produced movement, S moved his arm and the supporting swivel to which his arm was strapped through an arc of approximately 12°. In the exposure with passive movement, E moved the swivel on which S's relaxed arm was secured by straps through the same arc. To insure passive movement during exposure, S was given practice before the session in relaxing his arm as *E* moved it. Each of the two exposures lasted 6 min.; and during both of them, *S*'s hand, viewed through the mirrors, remained visible moving back and forth through the 12° arc in rhythm to a metronome set at 72 beats per min.

Views of the hand and its motion were identical in both the self-produced and the passive movement exposures. The only difference between these conditions was the type of movement—self-produced as opposed to passive movement. The re-afference hypothesis predicts that adaptation to the optically increased distance of the hand should occur only during self-produced movement. A shift of the post-exposure markings toward *S* was adaptive. He would initially have over-reached objects that he viewed through the mirrors had he attempted to localize them.

RESULTS

The mean shift following self-produced movement was 0.52 in. in the adaptive direction, while for passive movement the mean shift was 0.05 in. in the adaptive direction. The difference between the two mean shifts was significant at a level of confidence well beyond 1% (*t*-test for correlated scores). With self-produced movement, 14 of the 15 Ss showed adaptive shifts; for passive movement, only about half of the Ss showed adaptive shifts. The mean shift of 0.05 in. for passive movement was not significantly different from zero.

The results of this experiment support the proposition that re-afferent visual stimulation is a necessary condition for learning the new eye-hand coordination in the distance dimension. Comparable but ex-afferent stimulation resulting from passive movement did not produce significant shifts, although the optical information for *S* in both exposure conditions was the same. These results, or change in eye-hand coordination in the distance-dimension, can be added to the results of the studies previously mentioned which demonstrate the importance of re-afference in adaptation to disarrangement with other forms of sensory-motor coordination.

[4]

The Effects of Attitudes on Descriptions of Pictures

CLARENCE LEUBA and CHARLES LUCAS

This paper deals with the effects of three hypnotically induced attitudes—happiness, criticalness, and anxiety—upon observation and thought. Three Ss described a series of pictures when under the influence of these attitudes.

INTRODUCTION

Laymen as well as psychologists are well aware that attitudes, sets, moods, and other internal conditions may greatly affect both perception and thought. Nevertheless, it is only in recent years that a few experimental psychologists have brought the intellectual effects of these internal conditions under scientific scrutiny. When perception, memory, and intelligence are studied in the laboratory under simplified, objective, unemotional—almost inhuman—circumstances, factors like anxiety or resentment, which are of the highest importance in the everyday functioning of these processes, are overlooked. Gardner Murphy brings this out forcefully in his 1944 presidential address to the American Psychological Association (1945).

A new trend is indicated by Bartlett's (1932) and Rapaport's (1942) studies of the effects of attitudes and emotions on remembering, by Murray's (1933) study of the influence of fear upon children's estimates of the maliciousness of other personalities, and by Sanford's (1936, 1937) and Levine, Chein, and Murphy's (1942) investigations of the perceptual distortions produced by various degrees of hunger.

SOURCE: C. Leuba and C. Lucas, "The Effects of Attitudes on Descriptions of Pictures," *Journal of Experimental Psychology*, 1945, **35**, 517–524. Reprinted by permission of the American Psychological Association, C. Leuba, and C. Lucas.

Though projective techniques were originally developed to discover an individual's attitudes and other characteristics, they can also be useful for discovering the influence of known attitudes on perception and thought. Proshansky (1943) in a recent experiment found that liberals and conservatives, as determined by an attitude scale, could be reliably detected from their descriptions of suitably chosen pictures. In an unpublished experiment we found that, according to three judges, there were three times as many indications of anti-labor sentiments in the descriptions of six photographs of economic scenes by two anti-labor Ss as in those by two pro-labor Ss.

In these studies, the experimenters limited themselves to investigating the effects of already present attitudes on the description of pictures. Under ordinary circumstances the creation in the laboratory of the particular attitudes one wishes to study is difficult if not almost impossible. By using hypnosis, however, almost any attitude, set, or mood can be very readily created. In hypnosis the experimental psychologist has a technique for controlling variables in situations otherwise beyond the reach of psychological experimentation (Leuba, 1941). Erickson's investigations provide many illustrations of the successful use of post-hypnotic suggestions for the creation and study of such moods as resentment or jealousy (Erickson, 1939). Other investigators have been able to study the effects of hypnotically induced elation, depression, and hypochondria upon Rorschach records (Levine, Grassi, and Gerson, 1943, 1944).

Procedure

The present experiment involved the description of six pictures by three Ss when in each of three different moods: happy, critical, and anxious. The Ss—upperclass students in their early twenties, one man and two girls—were picked from a number of volunteers because of the ease with which they could be made to pass into the deepest stages of hypnosis.

The six photographs were chosen from current magazines. They showed young people of college age in a variety of situations, such as attending a seminar, digging in a swampy area, jitterbugging, engaging in battle activities, and lying on a sunny campus.

Each of the three Ss completed his portion of the experiment at one sitting and independently of the others. Each knew nothing of the experiment's purpose. The process of creating each of the three moods was done gradually, after the S had been deeply hypnotized. The final suggestion for the happy mood was as follows: "Now you are feeling very happy and you are in a cheerful and joyous mood. You feel as if everything is rosy and you are very optimistic. You have a comfortable feeling of well-being; nothing is worrying you. You feel perfectly at peace with everything and everyone. You are in a very happy, cheerful, and optimistic mood." It was noticed incidentally that facial expression tended to change with each mood.

After the S had described all six pictures, he was told to relax, close his eyes, and rest awhile. The happy mood was removed and the S was brought back to his "normal" hypnotic state. He was told that he would forget having seen the pictures just shown and that he would also forget what he had said about them. Then the S was gradually put into a critical mood. The final suggestion was: "Now you are very critical; you are quick to find fault and to condemn unfavorably. Your judgment of others is very harsh and severe. You see failings and faults very clearly. You are very critical and fault finding." The procedure of showing the six pictures, taking down the descriptions, then wiping out the induced mood, and suggesting amnesia for the pictures and for what had been said, was the same as for the happy mood.

The final suggestion in producing the last or anxious mood was: "Now you are quite anxious. You are disturbed over some possible misfortunes. You are disquieted and concerned as to something in the future. You are a little fearful and mildly alarmed. You have a feeling as if you were expecting something disagreeable to happen, yet were not sure that it would. You are quite anxious."

In each mood, Subject A was told to tell something about what was seen, as well as exactly what he saw in each picture. As a result A's reports tend toward accounts of what he thought about the situation pictured, or of what it reminded him. Subjects B and C were told to tell only what they saw in each picture; consequently they limited themselves more to what was actually in the picture and added less interpretative material. The pictures had no titles and were shown one by one always in the same order. None of the Ss showed any recollection of having seen the pictures while in the preceding mood. The E wrote down each S's description of each picture as he gave it (see tables on the following pages).

TABLE 1

Happy Attitude

Pictures	Subject A	Subject B	Subject C
I. Young people digging in a swampy area.	It looks like fun; reminds me of summer. That's what life is for: working out in the open, really living—digging in the dirt, planting, watching things growing.	Nice summer day. Working. Cool feet in water. Nice lot of food when they get through.	Boys and girls digging. Trees, stream, shovel. Mud all over them. Corn or wheat and shadow of a mountain in the background. Digging for irrigation or maybe planting something.
II. Colored people jitterbugging.	Having a good time. No matter what people say, they have a sense of rhythm. We whites miss that enjoyment; we worry too much.	Village—some night when they're really hot and having a good time. Just hilariousness.	Men and women jitterbugging. Zoot suit. Satin shorts on girl. They're having a good time; maybe a play of some sort.
III. Wounded man being carried on litter by soldiers to aeroplane.	Wounded soldier. Good thing men were there to help him and get him to a hospital. The men in this war are well taken care of.	Restfulness after a hard day's fight. Taking a guy back to safety from a battlefield.	Man being carried by litter bearers. Clouds and palms, canteen and flying jackets. Wounded being taken to a transport plane. Maybe Florida.
IV. Seminar around fireplace at faculty home.	Wonderful faculty group—it's wonderful, you don't find it everywhere. That's what's important in college; less booklearning.	Fireplace, home. All relaxed. Just a feeling of mellowness.	Woman reading to a group of people. Fireplace, clock, figures on mantle, books, fire. I like this. Very comfortable looking. Looks like fireplace at home.
V. Waist gunner in action in a bomber.	It's funny how they dress them up—protected from injury by machine. Now, they care more about the individual. Best possible working conditions.	Lot of work and exertion. Firing a gun in the heat of battle.	Looks like a monkey. Machine gun, empty cartridges. Oxygen mask, heavy clothing. Excellent composition, good photography.
VI. Four college men on sunny lawn typing, reading, listening to radio.	Before the war. Boys lying on campus listening to radio and reading. Not getting much done but having a good time. That's fun though.	Complete relaxation. Not much to do —just sit, listen, and relax. Not much at all to think about.	Sunbathers, radio, books, studying and typing in the sunshine. It must be a very warm and restful place.

TABLE 2

Critical Attitude

Pictures	Subject A	Subject B	Subject C
I. Young people digging in a swampy area.	Pretty horrible land. There ought to be something more useful for kids of that age to do instead of digging in that stuff. It's filthy and dirty and good for nothing.	Digging a ditch in slimy mud. Girls working there too, tsk, tsk. Looks like pretty hard work.	People digging and getting all dirty. The spade is not being held right. Don't look very clean. Stalks all battered down.
II. Colored people jitterbugging.	Negroes jitterbugging as usual; that's all they do. Unaesthetic; no one enjoys looking at it. Nothing good about it. They should be directed into other than useless activity.	One guy looks deformed. Seems to be having a good time though. Kid looks pretty young, Savoy or New York City. Probably all lit.	Bunch of crazy jitterbugs. He looks like a runt. Sort of silly because of the clothes and the movements they're making. All night binge. Don't like checks with stripes. Only one looks half decent.
III. Wounded man being carried on litter by soldiers to aeroplane.	Wounded or killed soldier; one more in a million who are just killing each other off. That's war, I guess. We must think it's fun or we wouldn't do something so useless as murder and destruction.	Wounded man being taken to safety, but a lot of good it does now. Looks as if they're in a hurry—must be pretty badly hurt. Must have been a tough scrap.	Fellows carrying away sleeping man. Movie set. Hands don't look natural or as if they're carrying something. The picture is artificial and was posed for.
IV. Seminar around fireplace at faculty home.	People sitting around talking. Sometimes we run up blind alleys arguing for the sake of argument.	Guy here looks disgusted. Grandmother looks bored. One gal is looking daggers. Grandpa doesn't look comfortable.	Woman reading to a bunch of unhappy people. Everything in the room is too formal. Reader is not comfortable. Girl with middy looks droopy. White-haired woman has a long face. I don't like picture.
V. Waist gunner in action in a bomber.	Typical example of man hiding away from himself. Closing himself in a factory. He doesn't know where he is going. Same thing every day and for what!	Having a hard time. Has been fighting steady for quite a while. Looks mean with goggles and maybe the guy he is shooting at looks just as mean.	Oh God! Man shooting gun. Why don't they pick up the shells? Messy. No room to move around.
VI. Four college men on sunny lawn, typing, reading, listening to radio.	Typical college campus. Everybody loafing. Typing a letter he doesn't need to type. Slacking on their work.	Someone ruining a good pair of pressed pants by lying down like that. They're unsuccessfully trying to study.	Somebody trying to get a tan, wasting time. Not comfortable. Tie coming undone, sole of shoe worn out. Messy. Leaves unraked.

TABLE 3

Anxious Attitude

Pictures	Subject A	Subject B	Subject C
I. Young people digging in a swampy area.	They're going to get hurt or cut. There should be someone older there who knows what to do in case of accident. I wonder how deep the water is.	Digging in a hurry to get rid of flood waters. Must be pretty important to get it done.	Burying something or digging something. Wide open field and mountain in the distance.
II. Colored people jitterbugging.	Look as though they're having a good time; it seems as though they shouldn't be because something may happen to their families.	Good time. I wonder how they'll feel tomorrow. Probably back to driving trucks.	People jitterbugging. I hope we don't look that way when we jitterbug. I don't like the picture.
III. Wounded man being carried on litter by soldiers to areoplane.	He is wounded and they're taking him to a plane but he's in bad shape and may not live even though the plane will rush him to a hospital.	Everybody in a hurry to get him back to safety. Must be emergency case, more so than usual. Man trying to act not too far gone but that doesn't mean he isn't.	Wounded man being carried off by buddies. Fliers, lots of boys like that. The man on the litter has a sweet face. I hate to have something like this happen; it frightens me.
IV. Seminar around fireplace at faculty home.	Mr. G. and some students. The picture is not right because Mr. G. isn't living any more. You never know when tragedy is going to hit.	Solving a big family problem. Everybody looking on. Anxious look on Grandmother and Sister. Thoughtful look on Grandpop's face.	Lot of people discussing. Lady reading to them. Somber atmosphere. It makes me feel as if I don't want to go to anyone's house.
V. Waist gunner in action in a bomber.	I wonder if it is safe—seems like the floor is badly cluttered. If anything happened I wonder if anyone would know. He might become tangled up in the rigging and be helpless.	Having a hard battle. Wonder if he'll win it. I bet he wonders what is going to happen to him.	Like monster from Mars. He's in a battle and perhaps he'll be killed. Don't like it because it reminds me of the war. Depressing.
VI. Four college men on sunny lawn typing, reading, listening to radio.	Boys relaxing on college campus. By now they may be overseas or wounded or dead. They never know whether they'll come through alive.	They're listening to a football game or world series. Probably a tight game. One guy looks as if his side wasn't winning.	Lot of men. Peaceful enough. I wonder if they want to come back, and what's going on in their minds. Are they fighting now?

101

RESULTS AND CONCLUSIONS

The induced attitudes are influential in determining what the S observes. In the happy mood, A describes picture IV as "a wonderful faculty group"; but in the anxious mood A's attention is focused entirely upon one recently deceased member of that group. The moods are much more noticeable, however, in their effects on the interpretation of what is observed. The meanings and feelings attached to the activities shown in the pictures and the probable causes and results of those activities are usually very different from mood to mood. In a happy frame of mind the Ss see the soldier in picture III "as being well taken care of," and as being taken "back to safety," or to a "transport plane." When in an anxious mood these same Ss say the soldier "is in bad shape," "may not live," "an emergency case," "it frightens me." After viewing picture VI, when in a happy mood, A says the boys are "lying on campus . . . having a good time." But when in a critical mood, A describes the boys as "loafing"; and when in an anxious mood, A thinks of them as maybe "overseas, or wounded, or dead." Attitudes exert a directive influence both on what is observed and on the train of thoughts suggested by the observations.

To gain a more objective appraisal of the extent to which the three attitudes actually influenced observation and thought, the 54 statements shown in the charts were typed on slips of paper and, after being thoroughly shuffled, were submitted to three judges. The instructions given the judges were: "The statements you have been given are brief descriptions of pictures. Indicate how many times, if any, each of these three attitudes or moods are expressed or implied in each statement: (1) HAPPINESS—cheerfulness, joy, optimism, well-being, satisfaction, approval of things as they are, contentment; (2) CRITICALNESS—fault-finding, condemnation, disapproval, dissatisfaction with things as they are; (3) ANXIETY—concern over the outcome of events, foreseeing unfavorable outcomes."

Descriptions made by the Ss when in a happy mood averaged, according to the three judges, 2.33 indications of happiness, .24 indications of criticalness and .13 indications of anxiety (Table 4). Under the critical mood, the average statement had three indica-

TABLE 4

Effects of Three Moods (Happy, Critical, and Anxious) on the Descriptions of Six Pictures by Three Subjects

Mood	Happy			Critical			Anxious		
	Happy	Critical	Anxious	Happy	Critical	Anxious	Happy	Critical	Anxious
Mean number of times each mood was indicated per picture	2.33 $\sigma = .96$	.24 $\sigma = .39$	.13 $\sigma = .17$	.09 $\sigma = .30$	3.15 $\sigma = 1.41$	.11 $\sigma = .23$	.17 $\sigma = .22$	.50 $\sigma = .57$	1.44 $\sigma = .78$
Statistical reliability of the differences between the means	$M_h - M_c = 2.09$ S.E.$_{\mathrm{dif.}}$ = .24; C.R. = 8.7			$M_c - M_h = 3.06$ S.E.$_{\mathrm{dif.}}$ = .35; C.R. = 8.7			$M_a - M_h = 1.27$ S.E.$_{\mathrm{dif.}}$ = .21; C.R. = 6.1		
	$M_h - M_a = 2.20$ S.E.$_{\mathrm{dif.}}$ = .23; C.R. = 9.5			$M_c - M_a = 3.04$ S.E.$_{\mathrm{dif.}}$ = .35; C.R. = 8.6			$M_a - M_c = .94$ S.E.$_{\mathrm{dif.}}$ = .25; C.R. = 3.8		

tions of criticalness and negligible indications of each of the other two attitudes. The effect of the anxious mood was not quite so clearcut: anxiety was indicated 1.44 times per statement, happiness .17 times, and criticalness .50 times. In every case the difference between the mean number of indications of the induced mood and the mean number of indications of each of the other two moods was statistically significant.

An anxious mood, as developed in this experiment, apparently tends to produce an appreciable number of remarks which three judges label as indicators of criticalness. The judges sometimes found it difficult to decide whether the remarks made during the anxious mood were critical, anxious, or neutral. The great majority of the descriptions written in the happy or critical moods, however, did not contain even a single remark which, according to the judges, was indicative of a mood other than the induced one. In some instances the mood exercised such a profound influence on perception that the picture would not be recognized from the description as the same one described in the other two moods.

These results would seem to indicate that (1) common sense and clinical insight are correct in assigning a major role to moods, feelings, and attitudes in the determination of intellectual processes; and that (2) even very brief descriptions of suitably chosen pictures show clearly the effects of a dominant attitude. Further experiments might be designed to discover what incidents typical of everyday life can create such powerful, directive attitudes, how these attitudes exercise their effects on perception and thought, and how these effects might be controlled. Hypnosis should prove an invaluable tool in creating the conditions necessary for such experiments.

[5]

The Honi Phenomenon: A Case of Selective Perceptual Distortion [1]

WARREN J. WITTREICH

Stability and continuity are the rule rather than the exception in ordinary perception. In spite of constantly shifting impingements upon its sense organs, the human organism does perceive the world in an orderly and sensible manner. However the facts of everyday perception are not explanations, and it is often only by deliberately distorting or changing the commonplace that we can shed any light on the processes which allow anything to become "commonplace" in the first instance. Perceptual distortions have therefore come to play an important role in the understanding of basic perceptual processes. Recently a number of devices have been developed which deliberately place cues in conflict to such an extent that strikingly dramatic perceptual distortions can be obtained.

A number of distorted rooms have been constructed in which the floor slopes up to the right of the observer, the rear wall recedes from right to left, and the windows are of different sizes and trapezoidal in shape. When an observer looks at any one of these rooms from a certain point with one eye the room appears normal or almost normal, as if the floor were level, the rear wall at right angles

[1] The work reported in this paper has been done under contract Nonr-27014 with Princeton University, a project initiated by the Professional Division, Bureau of Medicine and Surgery. The opinions expressed are those of the individual author and do not represent the opinions or policy of the Naval Service.

SOURCE: W. J. Wittreich, "The Honi Phenomenon: A Case of Selective Perceptual Distortion," *Journal of Abnormal and Social Psychology*, 1952, 47, 705–712. Reprinted by permission of the American Psychological Association and W. J. Wittreich.

to the line of sight and the windows rectangular and of the same size.[2]

One of these rooms has been built large enough so that people can enter the room and walk about in it. What the observer typically sees when he watches someone moving about in this room is a striking alteration in the observed individual's size. When standing in the corner to the observer's left, the person appears abnormally small; in the other corner he appears abnormally large. When walking from one corner to the other he appears to grow or shrink in size, depending upon the direction in which he is travelling. A smaller model of this room permits hands or faces to appear through the rear windows. As with the larger room, the hands or faces appear abnormally large or abnormally small, depending upon whether they are in the window to the observer's right or left.

The study to be reported here received its impetus from an unusual instance in which this typical pattern of observation was not reported. In 1949 a woman observed the faces of her husband and another man through the rear windows of the smaller room. The face of the other man was described as distorted in the usual manner, but no size changes whatsoever were reported for the husband; his face was described as being perfectly normal no matter which window it appeared in. Similar results were obtained in the large room. Again the other man was described in the usual manner: he appeared to grow or shrink and looked large or small, depending upon the corner in which he was observed. But again no such size changes were reported for the husband. No matter which corner he stood in, he was reported as looking perfectly norman—his usual size. This unusual observation was named the "Honi phenomenon" following the family nickname for the woman who first experienced and reported it.

This instance of a deviation from the typical pattern of observation of people in the room raises at least two specific questions. Is this observation simply a unique and isolated case or is it repro-

---

[2] These rooms were designed by Adelbert Ames, Jr., as part of a series of perceptual demonstrations. This description is modified from W. H. Ittelson and F. P. Kilpatrick, "Experiments in Perception," *Scientific American,* August 1951, **185,** 50–55. See also H. Cantril, *The Why of Man's Experience* (New York: Macmillan, 1950).

ducible with other individuals? What are the psychological conditions which account for such a performance?

This paper reports two experiments which answer the first question by producing the Honi phenomenon in unmistakable fashion with a number of other people. The obvious and outstanding relationship between the woman and her husband in the original situation was simply the fact that they were married. It should also be noted that both were over sixty years of age, and that he was a very distinguished man whom she greatly admired and to whom she was devoted. The assumption was made that if the phenomenon has been observed in this couple, it might very well be observed in certain other couples. A group of couples, the majority of whom had been married for a relatively short time, were selected as subjects primarily because of their availability and willingness to participate in the experiment.

In the first experiment an attempt was made to reproduce conditions under which the phenomenon had originally been observed, with the addition of needed experimental controls. All that was required of the S was a description of people observed in the room. It was assumed that if a description of what appeared to be a case of selective perceptual distortion had been obtained in the original situation, it could be obtained again. The prediction was simply that an individual, when observing both a stranger and his or her marital partner in the room, would report less distortion in the description of the marital partner than in the description of the stranger. The second experiment was an attempt to confirm what was found in the first experiment, and to obtain a quantitative measure of the difference in the relative distortion of the marital partner as compared to the stranger.

EXPERIMENT I[3]

Ten married couples provided a sample of 20 Ss in this experiment. At the time of the experiment six of the couples had been married less than one year. The remaining four couples had been married two, three and a half, five, and ten years, respectively. (See Table 1.)

[3] The experiment reported here is part of a larger pilot study which is reported in detail in F. P. Kilpatrick (ed.), *Human Behavior from the Transactional Point of View* (Hanover, N. H.: Institute for Associated Research, 1952).

Both the small and the large rooms were employed in this experiment. Both rooms were viewed with one eye only. With the small room, the S was asked to describe: (a) the room itself, (b) the hands of the experimenter placed through the rear windows, (c) a marble which ran across the room and gave the appearance of rolling uphill, (d) two situations with two people putting their heads through the rear windows: two strangers, and one stranger and the marital partner. (Each person was seen once in each window in each of the above situations.) Descriptions a, b, and c were requested primarily to see if the S was initially observing the room and objects in the room in the typical manner.

With the large room the S was asked to describe: (a) the room itself; (b) two situations with two people standing in the corners of the room: two strangers, and one stranger and the marital partner (each person was seen one in each corner in each of the above situations); and (c) two different people walking from the corner on the observer's left to the corner on his right and back again: a stranger, and the marital partner. The entire experiment was recorded on a wire recorder and transcribed.

RESULTS

An analysis was then made of each individual protocol to determine whether or not the S had spontaneously described a definite difference between the appearance of the marital partner and the appearances of both of the strangers, and whether this difference was in the predicted direction. Table 1 indicates that 6 out of the 20 Ss did report a difference in the expected direction in the small room and 7 out of 20 reported a similar difference in the large room. Not once did an S report a difference other than in the expected direction, i.e., not once was the marital partner described as being more distorted than either or both of the strangers. It is also of interest to note that, although the exact same people did not display the phenomenon in both rooms, there are a few striking cases of overlapping. Taking both situations together, it can be seen that at least one member of all the couples married under one year displayed the phenomenon to some degree in one of the two rooms, but, with a single exception, no member of the couples married over one year displayed the phenomenon. That single exception was a man married only two years.

Because of space limitations only selected portions of the individual protocols which contain material specifically relevant to the hypothesis will be presented. In reading these protocols it is worth

TABLE 1

Members of Married Couples Reporting Differences Between Marital Partner and Stranger When Observed in the Distorted Rooms

Couple	Length of Marriage	Difference in Appearance of Marital Partner and Stranger Reported by Husband or Wife *			
		Large Room		Small Room	
		Husband	Wife	Husband	Wife
1	3 mo.	x		x	
2	4 mo.	x		x	
3	7 mo.		x		x
4	3 mo.	x			
5	11 mo.	x	x	x	x
6	11 mo.			x	
7	2 yr. and 3 mo.	x			
8	3 yr. and 6 mo.				
9	5 yr.				
10	10 yr.				

* All differences reported are in the predicted direction, that is, marital partner distorting less than stranger.

noting a number of things. First of all, when an S reports a difference, he does so in a spontaneous manner, and he, himself, often appears to be struck by both the existence of this difference and the direction it takes. Second, it will be noted especially in protocols D and E in the large room that while the marital partner is maintaining some degree of constancy, the room itself is undergoing a process of increasing distortion. It appears almost as though the S is faced with a choice of distorting either the marital partner or the room, and he chooses to distort the latter. In all of the following protocols the marital partner is capitalized.

Small Distorted Room

A. Male, married 3 months: HER's looks bigger, but it doesn't look as much bigger than Bruce's did to yours although the windows look the same. It still looks bigger, but it doesn't look a great deal bigger. I think her head is bigger than Bruce's anyway naturally.

B. Female, married 7 months: I can't get over it. BOB's head appears to be far away and Bruce's head appears to be close, and BOB's head appears normal—uh, fairly normal—it's small, but it's more in proportion than Bruce's. That's all.

C. Male, married 4 months. BUNNY's head looks normal, but Bruce's head is much larger than you would expect. (Heads reversed) Now BUNNY's head is larger too, because of the size of the window; but not so much as it was the other way around. Bruce's head looked much larger than BUNNY's does.

D. Male, married 11 months: I guess your (NANCY) head has grown, but it hasn't grown much. You're (Bruce) like you were before, I guess. I guess NANCY is mostly bigger and Bruce looks smaller and NANCY's head is closer to me. (Heads reversed) That's right. That's amazing. Bruce's head looks larger but NANCY's looks—your (NANCY) head doesn't seem to have shrunk much. Bruce's head has grown.

E. Female, married 11 months: DAVID's head looks very big now. And Bruce's head looks the way it did before—when I looked at it the first time. Your head looks, darling; darling, you can't even get your head through that thing. But uh, I guess that's all. They both look in proportion. (Heads reversed) Gee. Golly. Well Bruce's head looks bigger now than it did the last time when he had his head on this side, and uh, and DAVID, I don't know about you. Your head looks big too, but you look normal in size—I think—whereas Bruce looks bigger than he is. I think that's all.

F. Male, married 11 months: Well, now it's reversed. As a matter of fact, Bruce looks larger in comparison to CHARLOTTE than CHARLOTTE did to Bruce in the previous situation. Other than size I can't see anything unusual. The faces appear normal, except Bruce seems closer and his face looks larger.

Large Distorted Room

A. Male, married 4 months: BUNNY's head looks about the size or smaller than this light bulb in the room, and Bruce's looks twice as large. Bruce looks like he's about—yeah, yeah he looks twice as tall as BUNNY. Twice as large, not only in height, but in width and everything. And uh—the left window's grown larger than the right. Bruce looks much—of course that is in relation to the people—the left window dwarfs BUNNY and the right window is dwarfed by Bruce. When I look at the feet, the slant isn't as pronounced as you might think it is. But it is a terrific slant. But it doesn't look too bad from here. (Change places) Oh geez. It's the same relationship, but BUNNY looks—Bruce looked much taller than he should have—and BUNNY looks about her size. I mean I could get in and stand beside BUNNY and look the same way she does—about the same size. Bruce looked much taller than BUNNY does, but Bruce at the same time looks as small as BUNNY did. The same holds with his head in relation to the light bulb and BUNNY's too. But the fact is, I think more of it is tied up with the fact that you know one person so much more, you know. I mean I can put myself in BUNNY's place and I know darn well that—uh—that's just about the size she would look. Doesn't make her look much larger, but Bruce it makes look smaller. Bruce looked like a giant standing in the corner and BUNNY looks normal, but at the same time I know darn well Bruce can't be that much smaller than BUNNY is. I mean on the street for example. She doesn't look like a giant and Bruce did. Put it that way. And now BUNNY looked like a midget and so does Bruce. Geez when I think back—even smaller he looks. I have to look at BUNNY in that corner again to tell you if Bruce looks smaller.

(Walking from corner to corner—marital partner) Well, BUNNY went from—everybody looks the same in that other corner—but BUNNY went from half her size to her normal size. I mean she looks normal now; she doesn't look any larger than she usually does. She got larger, but she didn't reach proportions which were beyond her normal. Geez, that's amazing. She doesn't start to get very much smaller until about two steps away from that very far corner there. All of a sudden she gets real small. And she's much further away now, too. Everybody looks the same size in that corner. (Stranger) Bruce gets larger and he gets larger than I know his size is, whereas BUNNY didn't. When he stands over in that other corner he looks the same size; I mean they both look very small. Now he looks larger than he usually does—you know—I mean when we're standing outside here. I notice his feet look larger than they did in the other corner—about size twelves up here and size fours down there. I guess he looks closer, but I can't remember. Yeah he does look closer than he did in the other corner. He got smaller again, but he didn't get smaller until he got practically two steps before the corner. Have him stand in the middle. Now he looks his normal size. Now he looks like BUNNY did when she was way up in that corner.

B. Female, married 11 months: DAVID? DAVID looks small too. He doesn't look—uh—really as small as Bruce did the last time, but he still looks considerably smaller than he is. And Bruce looks the way he did last time. Oh Bruce looks a lot bigger. DAVID's farther away though. (Change places) Hah. Hah. Hah. DAVID, DAVID—uh—darling you look pretty much normal except you aren't standing up in the corner as much there so you're closer to the middle of my eyes so you don't look tall. And Bruce looks very small. DAVID looks big.

(Walking from corner to corner—Stranger) Bruce is walking uphill. And now he is very tall, and he was small when he started. Now he's walking downhill, and now he's small again the way he started. (Marital partner) Well DAVID just walked uphill too, but he looks . . . I guess that's all. (He looks what?) Well, he looks more normal to me because I feel I'm a lot closer and it's more in proportion. Oh my, this is horrid. Well now he looks very far away. And he looks smaller, but he doesn't look awfully small. I mean he doesn't look awfully small. I mean he doesn't look—uh—sort of very little. He looks more average size only much farther away.

C. Female, married 4 months: Good night! Well, now the difference is tremendous because Bruce is so small. You see, I can't be objective about it. I know BOB is tall; therefore the difference between his and Bruce's height seems tremendous, more so that the other two. (Does BOB look taller than usual?) Yes, I think. Uh, that's hard to say; he doesn't look taller than usual. Not especially. It's just that Bruce looks so small. He's just minute. That's just about it.

D. Male, married 11 months: Bruce is large. NANCY is small. She is, how you say, Lilliputian. Well as a matter of fact the floor has become, it seems even more slanted. Her feet seem at more of a slant than the floor would indicate. You're (NANCY) just about belt size. Just an armful. You're quite small. When I look at NANCY without looking at Bruce, she looks normal, but when I look at Bruce, NANCY becomes smaller. NANCY is farther away too, and downhill. (Change places) Well, I'll be jiggered. NANCY looks, uh, this way, just looking at NANCY she looks quite normal. Just, I'd say, normal. Bruce looks smaller to NANCY. I think maybe Bruce looks smaller now than he did to Warren, though NANCY is farther away from the ceiling than Warren. Bruce looks very small and downhill too. I guess not as much. The same thing with his feet. His feet seem to be at more of an angle than the floor would indicate. When I look at them both, NANCY looks quite large, though further—no. NANCY looks quite normal actually.

E. Male, married 2 years: SALLY appears about normal to me. Of course Bob looks smaller. But SALLY doesn't look any different. When

Bob gets down there and SALLY gets up here it seems to change the appearance of the room slightly. The back wall there—it seems to make that window next to Bob seem a lot larger to me than the window on the right behind SALLY, a lot bigger than if I were just looking into the room without anyone in it.

F. Male, married 3 months: SHE looks about normal size. They look about equal in height. LOUISE is much—just bigger. HER face is larger, but in height SHE is about equal to Sally. Sally look about ⅖ her normal size.

G. Male, married 3 months: SHE not only goes from left to right, SHE grows big and SHE also comes a little bit towards me. SHE grows small but it looks so funny to hang on to things. SHE seems to go away from me just a little. Now SHE seems to be down and away from me just a little. Bruce looks the same as last time. When I look between windows he looks like a midget in a small room. When I look at him he seems like a guy standing in a far corner—not a normal far corner. Jan is very tall. SHE is right up to the ceiling. SHE seems to be more in proportion than Bruce.

EXPERIMENT II

As mentioned previously, this experiment was designed both to confirm the results of the first experiment and to provide a quantitative measure of the phenomenon. A number of assumptions underlie the procedure employed in this experiment. A person walking from the left to the right corner in the large room appears to go from very small, through a point of actual size, to very large. The reverse happens if he goes from the right to the left hand corner. If an S is set the task of subjectively determining the point at which the observed individual looks his normal size when walking from either corner, we would expect, on the basis of what was found in the first experiment, that a stranger would have to walk a greater distance from either corner than the marital partner in order to appear normal size. Conversely, since in either corner the marital partner appears normal, or more normal than a stranger, the partner will not have to move as far from that corner as the stranger will in order to appear of normal size. Furthermore, the magnitude of the difference between the distances traversed by the stranger and by the partner can be used as a quantitative measure of the magnitude of the phenomenon. At one extreme would be the case in which both stranger and partner had to walk the same distance; we would assume here that the phenomenon did not occur. The other extreme would be when the partner looked perfectly normal in the corner and did not have to move at all.

Hence the major prediction made in this experiment was that when the S is set the above task in the large room the point at which the marital partner appears normal will be significantly closer to the starting corner than will the point at which a stranger appears normal. It was also decided to specify the sex of the stranger, that is, provide a comparison of the partner with both a stranger of the same sex and a stranger of the opposite sex, in order to see if a sex difference might be observed. This specification as to the sex of the stranger had not been controlled in the first experiment; the strangers used were males.

In this experiment six married couples provided a total of twelve Ss. All couples but one had been married one year, and that couple had been married one year and three months.

Again, the S was first asked for a description of the empty room, observing the room from the specified point. Then an individual (either the partner or stranger) was introduced into the room and stood in one of the two corners. The S was asked what this person looked like. If the individual was described as being either too large or too small, S then received the following instructions:

When I tell (the individual in the room) to do so, he is going to walk slowly across the back wall. I want you to tell him to stop walking as soon as you feel that he looks his normal size, that is, the same size as if he were standing out here (outside of the room).

After E obtained assurance from S that he understood the instructions, S was asked to make two such judgments, once from the left corner and once from the right, for each of the following:

1 One person in the room only: (a) the marital partner, (b) stranger of same sex as the subject, and (c) stranger of opposite sex to that of S.

2 Two people in the room, each one standing in a corner, but only one person moving across the wall at a time: (a) the marital partner and stranger of same sex as S, (b) the marital partner and stranger of opposite sex to that of S, and (c) stranger of same sex and stranger of opposite sex.

Each judgment was recorded as the reading of the observed individual's position on a measuring tape which had been placed on the rear wall of the room. The tape read from left to right, and the readings were obtained directly from the tape by noting the point reached by the toe of the advancing foot, regardless of whether the individual had come from the left or right corner.

As soon as the S saw his or her marital partner in the room for the first time the experimenter asked for a further description of the room: "Before you go any further, I want you to describe the room to me again in as much detail as you possibly can." This was done to see if the introduction of the marital partner into the room would be accompanied by an increase in the distortion of the room itself as reported by S. Both descriptions of the room, before and after the introduction of the marital partner, were recorded on a seven-point distortion scale, which provided one point for each of the following which was described as being distorted in any way whatsoever: the floor, ceiling, walls, windows, doors, furniture, and miscellany (for example, the lighting fixture).

The readings on the tape measure provided the raw data for the experimental results. The S made a total of *18* judgments: *6* each for the marital partner, the stranger of the same sex, and the stranger of the opposite sex. Also available were the before-after distortion scores.

Because of the slant of the back wall it was necessary to convert the measurements in inches on the tape measure into angular displacement. This was done through the following steps:

1 The hypothetical center point on the rear wall was obtained by determining the point on the tape measure which was intersected by the median plane of the observer.

2 All readings were then converted into angular displacement from this center point, all readings to the right of center receiving a plus designation.

3 Reference points of 15° to both the left of the center point and to the right of the center point were selected. All readings coming from the left had a constant of plus 15 added to them; all readings coming from the right were first multiplied by minus 1, and then had a constant of plus 15 added to them. Consequently all minus numbers were cancelled out and comparable distance scores were obtained for all Ss coming from either corner. It should be pointed out here that, in terms of the original hypothesis, the actual distance traversed by each individual was not of primary interest. It was the difference between the points reached by different individuals that was of interest, and this difference remains unchanged no matter where the reference point is selected. The reference point is used for computational convenience.

4 For each individual observed by an S a mean position score was obtained by averaging the judgments (transformed as described above).

RESULTS

The results for the experiment are presented in Table 2. An examination of this table indicates that the basic hypothesis is borne

TABLE 2

**Differences in Mean Position Scores for Groups Observed:
Marital Partners, Strangers of Sex Opposite to Observer, and
Strangers of Same Sex as Observer**

Groups Compared	Respective Mean Position Scores		Diff	p
Stranger opposite sex–M.P.	17.09°	15.64°	1.45°	.001
Stranger same sex–M.P.	16.81°	15.64°	1.17°	.10
Stranger opposite sex–stranger same sex	17.09°	16.81°	.28°	.50

out: the marital partner was required to walk a shorter distance to be judged his or her normal size than either of the two strangers. The difference of 1.45° between the marital partner and the stranger of the opposite sex is significant at the .001 level of significance ($t = 3.48$). The difference of 1.17° between the marital partner and the stranger of the same sex is significant at the .10 level of significance ($t = 1.95$). The difference of .28° between the two groups of strangers is negligible ($t = 0.83$). The difference of 1.45° and 1.17° represent approximately 8 per cent and 7 per cent, respectively, of the observer's visual field within which the differences were observed, and correspond roughly to a six-inch difference on the tape measure.

An examination of the before and after room distortion scores, obtained as previously described, indicates that the mean room distortion score for the sample of Ss increased from 2.5 to 4.0 after the introduction of the marital partner, and this increase is significant at the .001 level of significance. This must be interpreted with care, however, since the nature of the cues offered by the introduction of *anyone* into the room would tend to make the room more distorted, certainly not less distorted. Yet it is interesting to compare the before-after distortion scores for the four Ss whose "measured distance" results are most in accord with the basic hypothesis with the four Ss whose "measured distance" results are least in accord with the hypothesis. The former group has mean distortion scores of 2.25 and 4.25, a difference of 2.00 in the predicted direction. The later group has mean scores of 1.75 and 2.50, a difference of only 0.75 in the predicted direction. Naturally such a small sample precludes drawing any definite conclusions from such a comparison, but it is suggestive of the possibility that the room distortion score does have meaning insofar as it aids in selecting those Ss whose reported perceptions are most in accord with the basic hypothesis.

D I S C U S S I O N

The phenomenon under study in this paper represents a particular instance of behavior in which an observer reports a lesser degree of distortion of his marital partner than of a stranger, when observed under conditions which normally produce visual distortion, for example, in the large and the small distorted rooms. This has been termed the "Honi phenomenon." The results from both experiments point to the conclusion that the Honi phenomenon is a reproducible instance of behavior which can be described adequately in both a verbal report and a quantitative measure and which is capable of having the variables associated with it roughly specified. This reported difference in distortion is capable of being quantified to the extent that a measurable difference can be obtained from the points on the back wall at which the marital partner and the stranger are judged to be of normal size when moving from either corner. In addition to the mere occurrence of the phenomenon, it should be pointed out that within the groups of S used marked individual differences were found which apparently were not due to chance factors, but seemed instead to be due to certain variables, as yet unspecified, contained within the situation itself.

The confirmation of the phenomenon plus the likelihood that the observed individual differences are real raise a very fundamental question which this paper cannot and does not attempt to answer. What are the psychological variables which can adequately explain both the phenomenon and the individual variations within the range of behavior provided by the phenomenon? The variable employed in both of the experiments is marriage, or various length of marriage. It may be assumed or inferred that this variable implies certain interpersonal, emotional, and valueful relationships between those married which cannot be assumed or inferred from the relationships of those not married. But the variable is itself a psychologically meaningless one, and no amount of assumption or inference can adequately specify those variables which are psychologically meaningful and which can adequately explain the observed behavior. Such information is obviously not contained in the experiments reported here, and only further experimentation can provide such information.

However, the experiments reported here do provide some hints as to possible hypotheses which can provide a basis for further experimentation. In the first experiment all of the instances of the phenomenon but one were reported by Ss who had been married less than one year. The differences obtained in the second experiment were from a sample of twelve in which all but two had been married less than one year. This would seem to suggest that the meaningful variables might be found through an examination of the relationships which are typical of the very earliest stages of marital life, although it must be remembered that the phenomenon was first observed in a couple that had been married over 25 years. It would also indicate that any explanation of the results reported here simply in terms of frequency would have to be rejected, since the results indicate a negative correlation between length of marriage and size of the reported or measured difference. In other words, the fact that one person has looked at another person more often does not explain the difference, and the results appear to contradict such an explanation.

Furthermore, it should be pointed out that any explanation of the experimental results must take account of something other, or something more, than just the nature of the retinal pattern and/or the nature of the stimulus configuration. The observer in this situation is faced with a definite conflict; apparently he cannot make both the room and the people in it look normal at the same time. Presumably one of the two has to be seen as distorted. The typical instance is to see the room as normal, and the people as distorted. In the atypical instance, the Honi phenomenon, the reverse appears to hold true: the room is seen as distorted and the marital partner as normal. The fact that both instances can and do occur indicates that in no sense can either instance be considered as "stimulus bound"; the stimulus and its retinal impingement are not, in and of themselves, an adequate explanation of the observed behavior.

It can readily be seen that the work reported here is entirely compatible with a great deal of experimental work which has been done within the framework of the so-called "transactional" viewpoint. As such, this experiment provides another instance in which a truly adequate and satisfactory explanation of the results must come from a consideration of the total "transaction," in which the perceiving mechanism and the stimulus configuration are merely integrally related parts, and in which the assumptions, needs, values, and purposes of the perceiver are equally as important.

SUMMARY

Two experiments were conducted in an attempt to see if an observable and measurable difference could be obtained in an observer's description of his marital partner as opposed to his description of a stranger, when both were observed in the large and the small distorted rooms.

The first experiment employed 12 couples, an N of 24, and utilized a purely verbal method of description. Both the large and small rooms were employed. A number of marked differences were obtained in which the marital partner was reported as being less distorted than the stranger. All but one of these differences were observed with Ss who had been married less than one year.

The second experiment attempted to quantify this difference by measuring the difference in the points on the back wall of the large room at which the marital partner and the stranger were judged to be of normal size when walking from either corner. Six couples, an N of 12, were employed as Ss. The obtained difference was significant and showed that the marital partner moved a shorter distance from either corner than the stranger to be judged normal.

It was pointed out that the variable employed in this experiment, marriage or length of marriage, was psychologically meaningless and could only suggest hypotheses for further experimentation which might provide a more satisfactory variable or set of variables. It was also noted that any adequate explanation must be provided in terms of something more than just a consideration of the perceiving mechanism and the stimulus configuration.

[6]
The Moon Illusion, II
IRVIN ROCK and LLOYD KAUFMAN

The horizon moon appears to be larger than the zenith moon; this is called the moon illusion. In the last issue of *Science* (Kaufman and Rock, 1962) a new technique for studying this illusion was described. It consists of a device which permits the observer to view a disk of light or artificial moon on the sky. The size of the disk can be varied. Using two such devices the observer can com-

FIGURE 1. The artifical moon as it would be seen by an observer looking at the horizon through the combining glass, with one eye. The observer would view the scene directly with his other eye; thus any disturbing images of the edges of the combining glass, or of the clamp, would tend to be washed out.

SOURCE: I. Rock and L. Kaufman, "The Moon Illusion, II," *Science*, 1962, 136, 1023–1031. Reprinted by permission of the American Association for the Advancement of Science and I. Rock.

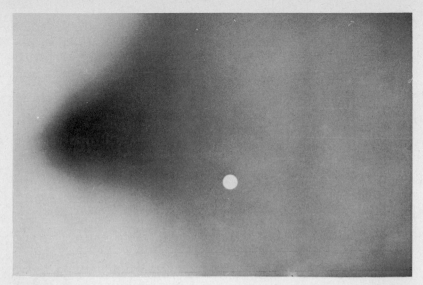

FIGURE 2. The artificial moon as it would be seen by an observer looking at the zenith through the combining glass. The dark regions in the two pictures are an out-of-focus image of the clamp that holds the combining glass.

pare a standard disk set in one position of the sky (for example, on the horizon) with a variable disk set in another position (for example, at the zenith) (see Figures 1 and 2). The variable selected by the observer to match the standard in size gives a measure of the magnitude of the illusion. Experiments carried out with this technique failed to support the earlier finding that the illusion was based on the elevation of the eyes with respect to the head (Holway and Boring, 1940). It was also shown that the illusion was not based on changes in the color or brightness of the moon. Here, in part 2, we discuss work on the apparent-distance hypothesis.

THE APPARENT-DISTANCE HYPOTHESIS

We are now ready to consider the hypothesis that the illusion is based on the sense of great distance which the observer has when viewing the moon directly above the horizon. This sense of distance is created by the terrain, which for present purposes, may be defined as a stimulus which yields the impression of a plane receding from the observer. (It should be noted here that the sense of distance or apparent distance need not necessarily correspond to the subject's report of distance. This point was discussed earlier [Kaufman and Rock, 1962] and is covered in more detail later.) We have already shown that the moon illusion cannot be explained by factors operating in complete darkness, even when the moons compared are at optical infinity. This finding can be taken as supporting the apparent-distance hypothesis, because, in the case of the ordinary illusion, the zenith moon is essentially a disk at optical infinity surrounded by a homogeneous field. Therefore, in effect, the dark-field experiments may be said to eliminate the visible terrain in viewing the horizon moon, and in so doing, to abolish the illusion.

THE EFFECT OF OBSCURING THE TERRAIN FROM VIEW. We also tested this deduction somewhat more directly by obscuring the terrain under outdoor conditions. The observer compared an artificial moon set near the horizon with another artificial moon seen through a ⅜-inch aperture in a large cardboard mounted in front of the second instrument. The latter "reduction moon" was located approximately 10° above the horizon to make sure that no part of the terrain would be seen through the opening. The observer was required to place his head against the cardboard and look through the aperture at the moon reflected by the combining glass. Because the reduction moon could be viewed with only one eye, the observer was required to view the unobstructed horizon moon with one eye. The observer also compared the reduction moon with the (monocularly viewed) zenith moon. For this purpose the assembly for viewing the unobstructed moon was tilted back on the tripod so as to locate the disk in the zenith. With these exceptions the procedure for each of these comparisons was identical to procedures followed previously. Ten male students from Hofstra College were used as observers. They viewed the scene across Mitchel Air Field; the sky in that direction was clear throughout the afternoon of the experiment.

The mean ratio obtained in a comparison of the normal moon with the reduction moon was 1.34 (standard deviation, 0.08), where the reduction moon was considered to be the zenith moon of the previous experiments. In other words, we obtained an illusion with both moons in a horizontal direction merely by eliminating the visible terrain in viewing one of them. Moreover, the magnitude

of the effect was about the same as that obtained, with other subjects, for the ordinary moon illusion for this same scene (1.38),
under similar sky conditions. [It is worth noting in passing that this
result, obtained with monocular viewing, fails to support the conclusion of Taylor and Boring (1942) that binocular vision is essential for a moon illusion. We know of two monocular individuals
who report experiencing a moon illusion. Binocular viewing should
not be crucial, according to the apparent-distance hypothesis, because the important stimulus to distance, the terrain, is received
monocularly.] The mean ratio obtained in a comparison of the reduction moon with the zenith moon was 0.99 (standard deviation,
0.04). There is thus no illusion when the terrain is blocked from
view.

REVERSAL OF THE ILLUSION BY MEANS OF MIRRORS. If the presence of the visible terrain is indeed crucial, as the foregoing evidence suggests, it should be possible to reverse the illusion by giving
the zenith moon a terrain, so to speak, and at the same time depriv-
ing the horizon moon of its terrain. In other words, if one were to
see the zenith moon over a horizon at the end of an apparent terrain, it should appear larger than a moon viewed horizontally but
not in connection with a terrain—a moon surrounded on all sides
by sky.

We achieved this condition by requiring the subject to view each
artificial moon through a right-angle prism, which is essentially a
mirror at a 45° angle to the line of sight. The observer is seated with
his back to the terrain scene he is to view. To see one moon he tilts
his head and eyes upward to 90° so as to view the scene through
the prism. The prism opening is 5¼ inches long and 1⅛ inches high.
The observer places his eye as close as possible to the prism. Directly
behind the prism and off to one side is the small combining glass
which reflects an artificial moon so as to make it appear within the
mirrored scene. The observer then sees the terrain stretching vertically upward. The artificial moon is made to appear on top of the
perceived horizon. To see the other moon, the observer looks through
a second prism (below a combining glass), which reflects the zenith
sky in a horizontal direction. Hence he sees the artificial moon
straight ahead, in a horizontal direction, but instead of seeing terrain
below it he sees sky surrounding it.

This particular experiment was performed on the roof of the Graduate School of Education Building of Yeshiva University, on 57th Street in Manhattan. Because it was not necessary to remove the apparatus daily, as was the case on the Hofstra campus, the instruments were attached to a wooden framework. The zenith unit was clamped to a horizontal board, which the observer could view

FIGURE 3.   One of the scenes used to study the moon illusion. One moon was located between the buildings directly over the horizon. The other was placed in the zenith sky. When this scene was inverted by means of prisms the illusion was considerably reduced. Note the reduction in the impression of depth when the scene is viewed upside down.

from a sitting position. The horizontal unit was attached to a vertical board, which the observer could view from the same sitting position. The framework provided a firm anchorage for the right-angle prisms used in this experiment. The view facing east from the roof included the street, lined with buildings, and the horizon at the end of 57th Street, which was at a distance of well over a mile (Figure 3).

Ten students of Yeshiva University were used as subjects. To compare the illusion obtained with the mirrors with that obtained under normal conditions, we had the subjects of the mirror experiments view the same scene without the mirrors. This control condition indicated the magnitude of the illusion to be expected under conditions that were comparable except for the use of mirrors. Half of the subjects viewed the mirror scene one day and the regular scene the following day. For the other half the order was reversed. The procedure of measurement was otherwise identical to that employed in the previous experiments.

The mean ratio for the mirror experiment was 1.37 (standard deviation, 0.28) and for the control variation, 1.56 (standard deviation, 0.25). The difference is statistically significant. Because the scene of a city street with buildings surrounding the horizon sky might be considered a special case (and certain facts support this view), the experiment was also performed at the Hofstra College site, with minor variations in the physical arrangement of the apparatus. For nine subjects the mean ratio was 1.34 (standard deviation, 0.25). This value is significantly lower than the ratio obtained without mirrors at the same location and under similar cloud conditions—namely, 1.54 (standard deviation, 0.19). The ratios obtained with and without reversal are strikingly similar in the two experiments.

The results thus show that we were successful in reversing the illusion, although the magnitude of the effect obtained is not as great as that of the ordinary illusion. Does this mean that the visible terrain is not the whole story—that some other factor, such as angle of regard, also plays a role? It must be borne in mind that, from the standpoint of an angle-of-regard theory, not only should the illusion not have been reversed but the true horizon moon should have continued to appear larger. Hence, if both factors were operating and were of equal strength, we should expect them to cancel each other out, because they are in opposition. The obtained reversed ratios of 1.37 and 1.34 in the two experiments can then only mean that if an angle-of-regard factor were involved, it must have exerted only a very weak influence. More plausible, therefore, in the light of this reasoning and all the evidence cited earlier against an angle-of-regard theory is the conclusion that the reduction in the size of the visible field, as the observer looked through the tank prism, reduced the impression of depth yielded by the scene. (Also, the frame of the prism may have provided a constant reference system for judging visual angle.) Moreover, looking up at a landscape aligned perpendicular to gravity is unnatural, and this may have been a factor. If these conjectures are correct, one may say that the effect nevertheless obtained is very impressive indeed.

It seems clear, then, that it is the presence of terrain in one case and the absence of terrain in the other that is the major factor in the moon illusion. But the objection can justifiably be made that this in itself is not sufficiently analytical proof of the apparent-distance hypothesis. Perhaps the presence of the terrain stimulus pattern adjacent to a moon creates the effect for reasons other than the pattern yields a sense of great distance. Although there may be no obvious rationale for such an effect, it still must be established that it is the distance aspect of the terrain stimulus which is crucial.

AN INVERTED TERRAIN. It is a fact known to psychologists in the field of perception that an inverted photograph of a landscape often loses much of its effect of depth (Figure 4). Although this is as yet unexplained, there is no question about the fact, and we decided to make use of it to test the apparent-distance hypothesis. If an observer were to view an inverted scene he would have a sense of less distance to the horizon moon than he has in viewing the scene without inversion. Hence, according to the apparent-distance hypothesis, the illusion should be diminished. Yet the terrain stimulus pattern would remain adjacent to the horizon moon, and thus, if the crucial factor is some aspect of the terrain pattern other than distance, the illusion created should be undiminished.

The observer viewed the 57th Street scene through two large Dove prisms, each $1 \frac{9}{16}$ by $1 \frac{1}{16}$ inches in cross section, mounted side by side directly in front of the combining glass. The subject sat with his eyes close up against the prisms. The prisms were mounted in a thick cardboard in which a hole had been cut equal in size to the cross-sectional area of the two prisms combined. The cardboard thus surrounded the prisms on all sides, serving as a shield which prevented the observer from seeing the scene in any way except through the prisms. He viewed the zenith moon normally, without prisms. To compare results of observations with and without inversion of the scene, a control condition was included in which the observer viewed the scene through an aperture equal in size to the two prisms combined—that is, an aperture 3 ⅛ by 1 1/16 inches. Four subjects were tested first under the experimental condition and six subjects first under the control condition. Otherwise the procedure was identical to the measurement procedures described previously.

The mean ratio for ten naive subjects was 1.66 (standard deviation, 0.32) without the prisms [1] and 1.28 (standard deviation, 0.17) with the prisms. (Three of the control subjects selected apertures at the upper end of the series, so the mean ratio of 1.66 is somewhat conservative.) These two values differ significantly from one another, and the second differs significantly from unity. Thus there are two conclusions to be drawn: (1) the inversion of the scene does very appreciably reduce the moon illusion, and (2) there is still an illusion even with inversion.

The first conclusion provides important support for the apparent-distance hypothesis. The second leaves us with an unsolved problem. It is probable that the inverted scene does not completely eliminate a sense of depth. This conclusion is especially plausible in the case of this particular scene, which contains a perspective pattern derived from the vertical lines of buildings as well as one derived from the horizontal elements along the ground plane. The perspective based on the vertical elements is not changed with inversion. Furthermore, there are other possible cues to the scene's true depth, such as monocular parallax. We retained some sense of depth in viewing the inverted scene. But there is another factor to be considered in the case of this particular scene. The moon is seen between tall buildings. Thus, it is framed on three sides, and this frame of reference might very well affect the moon's apparent size

[1] The high ratio obtained in the noninversion condition despite the restricted field of view of the aperture seems to contradict the explanation offered for the reduced illusion in the mirror experiment. This is not necessarily a contradiction, however, because the aperture is not as deep as that of the right-angle prism and allows the observer to see more of the foreground. Also, different groups of subjects were used in the two control experiments, and the cloud conditions were probably not identical.

(Rock and Ebenholtz, 1959). Some additional evidence on this point was obtained in experiments conducted in the laboratory with slides of outdoor scenes. In one such experiment a slide of the 57th Street scene was shown, and, as a control, a slide of a pattern virtually identical to that scene with respect to line elements but drawn so as not to convey a sense of three-dimensionality. The moon seen in the control slide was, therefore, also framed on three sides. This slide yielded an illusion ratio close to 1.2, quite similar to the ratio obtained with the inverted scene. Such a relational effect would be in no way changed by inversion of the scene. Thus, it is possible that the slight illusion obtained with the inverted scene is due to a residual depth impression or a relational effect of the surrounding buildings, or both. It would be instructive to repeat this experiment with slides of a more typical landscape, such as the scene at Hofstra College, which does not produce a framing effect.

Various authors have commented on the apparent destruction of the moon illusion that occurs when an observer views the horizon moon between his legs. Boring interpreted this as evidence supporting the angle-of-regard hypothesis. Our finding of a diminution of the illusion with an inverted scene (which does not involve any change in angle of regard) suggests an alternative explanation: inverting the head brings about an inversion of the retinal image, and the latter inversion, for whatever reason, diminishes the impression of depth yielded by the landscape. (It might also be pointed out that looking between one's legs inevitably lowers the observer's vantage point. Looking at the terrain from a point nearer the ground would also decrease the apparent distance to the horizon.)

VARIATION OF DISTANCES AND CLOUD CONDITIONS. It should follow from the hypothesis under investigation that the moon illusion would increase with apparent distance to the horizon. We therefore performed an experiment in which the illusion was compared for two scenes which differed substantially in the impression of distance to the horizon. One scene extended north from the Hofstra College campus and encompassed Mitchel Air Force Base; for this scene the apparent distance from the viewing point to the horizon was roughly 2 miles. The other scene was 30° west of the first. In this direction trees and shrubbery obscure the horizon at a distance of about

2,000 feet. Thus, the apparent distance ($D1$) for the first scene was much greater than that for the second ($D2$).

Another factor which might conceivably contribute to the differential impression of distance to horizon and zenith is the presence of clouds, as Helmholtz (1925) and others have speculated. In fact, Miller (1943) found the half-arc angle to vary inversely with the degree of cloudiness. We therefore decided to include a test of the effect of cloudiness on the illusion. This was done by testing different subjects on totally clear days, on totally overcast days (with structured stratocumulus cloud coverage), and on days with broken coverage (that is, with clouds predominantly cumulus, and with coverage judged to be between 0.3 and 0.7). It was expected that the illusion would be maximal on totally overcast days, minimal on totally clear days.

The design of this experiment involved testing subjects under six sets of conditions—combinations of the two apparent distances and the three types of cloudiness. It was not feasible to use subjects as their own controls by testing them under all conditions of cloudiness, because we obviously could not manipulate the cloud conditions at will (although we were able to test some subjects for both distances). Altogether, 55 Hofstra College students, male and female, served as subjects, 20 on overcast days, 20 on days with broken cloud coverage, and 15 on clear days. Half the subjects tested under overcast and broken-cloud conditions viewed the horizon moon over scene $D1$ and half over scene $D2$. Five of the subjects tested under the clear-sky condition viewed the moon over both scenes, and the remaining ten viewed it over one or the other. In this experiment each subject made two ascending and two descending series of matches for each moon that served as the standard. The procedure followed was otherwise the same as in the other experiments. The zenith moon was set at an elevation of 80°.

The results are given in Table 1 in terms of the average ratios for each of the six subgroups and for overall distance and overall cloud conditions. The data of Table 1 reveal an increase in the illusion with increasing cloudiness and a greater illusion with greater apparent distance to the horizon ($D1$). An analysis of variance shows that the cloud-condition ratios differ significantly, as do the distance-condition ratios. (As noted above, five of the subjects were tested for $D1$ as well as for $D2$. An additional four subjects were also tested for both $D1$ and $D2$. In all these tests the sky was clear. For eight of the nine subjects the illusion was larger for $D1$. For the ninth

TABLE 1

Average Illusion Ratios for Various Distances and Cloud Conditions
(Ten Observers for Each Cloud-and-Distance Condition)

| Distance | Cloud Condition | | | | | | Overall |
| | Clear | | Broken | | Overcast | | |
	Mean	SD	Mean	SD	Mean	SD	(Mean)
Near ($D2$)	1.28	0.17	1.35	0.27	1.45	0.21	1.36
Far ($D1$)	1.40	.22	1.54	.19	1.58	.28	1.51
Overall	1.34		1.45		1.52		

subject the illusion was the same for $D1$ and $D2$. The average for these nine subjects was 1.25 for $D1$ and 1.14 for $D2$.) These results support the apparent-distance hypothesis and confirm Helmholtz's speculations on the role of cloudiness, as well as the findings of Miller, Neuberger (1952), and others.

ERROR OF THE STANDARD

In most of the experiments reported in this article the illusion obtained was greater when the horizon moon was the standard than when the zenith moon was the standard. This is apparent in Table 2, where the results are given separately for the two cases for all experiments. Only in the eye-elevation experiment in which the "binocular" collimator was used, and in the experiments in which no illusion was obtained, does this difference fail to appear. We would be inclined to believe that the exceptional result in the former case is a function of the slight differences in the apparatus were it not for the fact that in other experiments, not reported in this article, in which the binocular collimator was employed a similar effect was obtained. The absolute magnitude of the effect is considerably

TABLE 2

Average Ratios Given Separately for the Horizon Standard and the Zenith Standard

Condition	Horizon Standard	Zenith Standard	Average
Eyes raised versus eyes level			
Eyes raised	1.46	1.51	1.48
Eyes level	1.47	1.46	1.46
Both moons in same region of sky			
	1.07*	1.01†	1.04
Dark field			
	1.03	1.03	1.03
Color (red and white horizon moons combined)			
	1.49	1.23	1.36
Brightness			
	1.53	1.28	1.40
Obstructed versus unobstructed terrain			
	1.41	1.27	1.34
Obstructed terrain versus zenith			
	1.02	0.97	0.99
Mirror reversal			
57th Street	1.54	1.20	1.37
Control	1.79	1.33	1.56
Hofstra	1.49	1.20	1.34
Inverted terrain			
Prisms	1.37	1.19	1.28
Control	1.95	1.38	1.66
Various distances and cloud conditions			
Long distance (D1):			
Clear	1.56	1.23	1.39
Broken	1.75	1.33	1.54
Overcast	1.73	1.43	1.58
Short distance (D2):			
Clear	1.40	1.15	1.27
Broken	1.44	1.25	1.34
Overcast	1.61	1.28	1.44

* Moon viewed with eyes level taken as the standard.
† Moon viewed with eyes raised taken as the stantard.

smaller than that of the moon illusion itself. A rough approximation is yielded by dividing by 2 the average difference between

$$\frac{\text{Variable zenith setting}}{\text{Standard}}$$

and

$$\frac{\text{Standard}}{\text{Variable horizon setting}}$$

for those experiments where such an effect occurred. This yields a value of approximately 15 percent; that is, a comparison object would have to be made 15 percent greater in size than a standard object if only such an error were operating.

One way of viewing this finding is in terms of a tendency to over-estimate the standard; this tendency has in recent years been discovered by others working on size judgments and called "the error of the standard" (Piaget and Lambercier, 1956). In our experiments this tendency would increase the magnitude of the illusion when the horizon moon is the standard because it makes the already phenomenally large moon seem even larger. It would decrease the magnitude of the illusion when the zenith moon is the standard because it makes the smaller-appearing zenith moon seem larger, thus offsetting the illusion to some extent. This constant error might be considered to be a positive time error for size except for two considerations. (1) It has not been experimentally demonstrated that the error is a function of the order of presentation, only that it is associated with the stimulus made to serve as the standard. In fact, in many of our experiments the subject was allowed to check the standard after setting his variable. (2) The effect does not seem to appear in our experiments when the moon illusion itself does not appear, although this should provide an ideal opportunity for observing the operation of a time error if one exists.

The fact that, in our experiments, the effect does not seem to be present unless the moon illusion itself is present suggests another interpretation relating to certain phenomenal differences between the horizon and the zenith moons. We will therefore return to this problem.

DISCUSSION

METHODOLOGY. Since our results on the matter of eye elevation fail to substantiate previous findings, the difference in method employed becomes crucial. In addition to the points made earlier concerning our reasons for dissatisfaction with the method used by Boring and his associates, we would like to make a comment concerning our method. Assuming that viewing the sky through glass does not affect the results—an assumption that we think justified (to which we may now add the observation that in our dark-field experiment the observer does not see the apparatus and is looking directly at the artificial moon—we believe we have duplicated the conditions of the moon illusion in nature)—comparison of a moon in one region of the sky with a moon in another region. Our observers merely have to compare one moon with the other, they do not have to compare either moon with anything else. The one remaining difference between our experimental conditions and the conditions in daily life is that of immediate versus delayed comparison. But this is a difference which we deliberately introduced in order to eliminate any dependence on memory; impressions of the moon illusion in daily life may be somewhat spurious because of the unknown role of memory.

In support of our contention that we have duplicated the conditions found in nature, we performed an experiment in which three observers were asked to compare the *real* horizon moon (viewed over the ocean) with our artificial moon pointed at the zenith. The average illusion ratio obtained was 1.83, a value slightly inflated by the lack of a control for an error of the standard. Observations by these same subjects yielded no illusion ratio whatever when the artificial moon was pointed at the horizon but 40° to one side of the real moon. In the latter comparison the subjects selected an aperture identical to the one they had selected when the artificial moon was directly superimposed on the real moon. In other words, the aperture of our apparatus, known to subtend approximately the same visual angle as the real moon, yielded a phenomenal disk equal in size to the phenomenal moon when the two were seen at the same elevation. But when the aperture was viewed at the zenith it appeared much too small. These checks demonstrate the phenomenal equivalence of our artificial moon and the real moon.

If our reasons for questioning the method used by Boring and his associates are valid, and if our method is indeed a duplication of the illusion as it exists in nature, two problems remain unsolved: how their observers were able to arrive at a satisfactory match, and why these matches revealed a moon illusion dependent on eye elevation. It is a fact worth noting that, for the most part, either Boring, his colleagues, or other persons familiar with the problem under investigation served as subjects. A more serious contradiction exists, however—one between our findings and those of Holway and Boring in experiments carried out with their direct-comparison (reflected mirror-image) method. The contradiction is serious because, as we have noted, the essential conditions of the moon illusion are successfully duplicated in this method. Boring and his colleagues obtained only a verbal estimate of the difference in size, and again it should be noted that the observers were familiar with the problem under investigation. The same is true for findings of Holway and Boring concerning an illusion of the sun seen through dense filters. Nor can we shed any light at this time on Schur's findings of an illusion based on differences in perceived direction inside darkened buildings (1925). As already noted, it would seem that our dark-field experiment is the ideal test for such an effect, yet the result we obtained was only negligible.

Very recently Leibowitz and Hartman reported an experiment (1959) in which subjects in a darkened theater made size comparisons of disks seen overhead with disks seen straight ahead. The disks were 35 feet away. The overhead disk was underestimated by 19.1 percent by adults and by 32 percent by children of 5 to 8 years of age. We are at a loss to explain this finding, in the light of our planetarium and dark-field experiment, except to note that some stray light from the projector enabled the observers to detect the outlines of chairs on the ground,[2] and that the cues for distance in the horizontal direction were thus probably better than those in the vertical direction. There is nothing but empty space between observer and overhead disk. (The same point is relevant to Schur's

[2] Personal communication, 1961.

experiment.) Leibowitz and Hartman obtained similar results out-doors with a disk suspended outward from the roof of an 85-foot building. The latter finding could also be a function of the superior cues for distance along the ground or a function of the "framing" of the horizontal disk by the wood backing and by objects behind it.

THE CONTEXT EFFECT. It seems quite clear from the various experiments reported here that a visible terrain is essential for the appearance of the illusion. Have we demonstrated that the terrain produces the illusion because it increases the perceived or registered distance of the horizon moon? There were two findings in support of this conclusion: (1) when the horizon appeared farther away the illusion increased; and (2) the illusion decreased when the terrain pattern was inverted, presumably because the impression of depth decreased. Logically the only alternative to the distance hypothesis is the theory that the terrain pattern, as a two-dimensional structure or context, increases the apparent size of a disk seen adjacent to it as compared to the apparent size of a disk seen within a homogeneous surround. On the face of it this alternative is not a particularly plausible one, since the typical terrain lies entirely to one side of the moon—that is, it does not frame the moon except in the case of scenes containing tall buildings or the like. It is unlikely that, under these circumstances, such a context effect, even if it existed, could approach in magnitude the moon illusion obtained. In any event, we ruled out this possibility in experiments in which we sought to achieve an illusion indoors by means of slides of terrain patterns. On the whole, only a negligible illusion was obtained when a disk seen above the terrain on the screen was compared with a disk seen within a homogeneous surround. No illusion at all was obtained when a control slide was substituted which duplicated the terrain pattern in all structural essentials but which was deliberately drawn so as not to yield an impression of depth. If the moon illusion is a function of such a context effect, we can see no reason why it should not be easily created in the laboratory. On the other hand, if it is a function of apparent depth, one can readily see why it is difficult to create it in the laboratory. Hence, we may consider these negative results still a third piece of evidence in support of the distance interpretation of the role of the terrain.

THE SIZE-DISTANCE INVARIANCE HYPOTHESIS. We turn now to

certain theoretical questions bearing on the apparent-distance hypothesis. As noted earlier, there has been considerable dissatisfaction in the last few years with explanations of size perception based on the taking into account of distance—or with what is being called the size-distance invariance hypothesis. We need not repeat our reasons for questioning the basis for this dissatisfaction. In any case, it is not clear whether those who question the invariance hypothesis wish to argue that phenomenal size is not at all a function of distance or merely that the precise nature of the function is not known. As far as the moon illusion is concerned, our claim is not that every increment in perceived or registered distance will necessarily yield some proportional increment in the phenomenal size of the moon but merely that, in a gross way, the horizon moon appears larger because it appears much farther away, or that a very-distant-appearing horizon moon looks larger than a not-so-distant-appearing horizon moon.

Recently the so-called paradox concerning the relative apparent distances of the two moons first pointed out by Boring has been cited as further evidence against the invariance hypothesis (Epstein, Park, and Casey, 1961). The horizon moon allegedly appears nearer, not farther away. We dealt with this problem earlier in terms of certain logical considerations and cited experimental evidence in support of our position (Kaufman and Rock, 1962), but it might be well to reiterate our belief that what is crucial is not distance as judged but distance as registered by the nervous system on the basis of certain stimuli. Woodworth and Schlosberg have made this very point in discussing the seemingly paradoxical results of stereoscopic studies of changes in convergence. They proposed a solution "in terms of a multilevel view of perception." [3] "We may assume" they state, "that convergence and the resulting appropriate distance are registered at a low level of the perceptual sequence and serve as cues for judgments of size, although the cues themselves are not directly available through introspection. The size judgments then serve as cues for another judgment of distance, which may conflict with the lower-level cue." This is precisely the way in which we have tried to deal with the paradox reported by Boring. We propose

[3] R. S. Woodworth and H. Schlosberg, *Experimental Psychology* (2d ed.; New York: Holt, 1954), p. 477.

that changes in phenomenal size may be a better index of changes in registered distance than of reportable changes in perceived distance. To support the invariance hypothesis one need only show that specifiable changes in registered distance (as indicated by convergence, accommodation, and so on) yield predictable changes in phenomenal size; not that changes in phenomenal or judged distance yield predictable changes in phenomenal size.[4] Nevertheless, in the case of the moon illusion, when judgment can be eliminated as a factor by removing the moon from view, observers then do report the horizon *sky* to be farther away.

STIMULUS CORRELATES OF DISTANCE. We have not tried to tackle the question of what the important stimulus correlates of distance are in the case of the moon illusion, except indirectly. The importance of clouds, and of scenes which allow one to view the horizon at a very great distance, suggest that configurational properties of the stimulus are crucial, because physiological correlates cease to be important at great distances. By *configurational* we mean relationships within the stimulus pattern, such as perspective, interposition, and the like.[5] The effect of inverting the scene supports this line of reasoning. In any case, we can rule out convergence and accommodation, because these adjustments are the same for horizon and zenith moons in daily life as well as in our experiments. One can easily eliminate other nonconfigurational correlates of distance perception, such as retinal disparity and movement parallax, by viewing the real moon with one eye and with the head stationary; an observer viewing it in this way still seems to obtain a substantial illusion—at least we do. If this reasoning is correct, and if, as is plausible, the configurational correlates are a product of experience, then the illusion itself would be indirectly dependent on experience.

THE CONSTANCY FUNCTION. In one respect the apparent-distance hypothesis oversimplifies the problem of the moon illusion. On the

---

[4] We are not taking the position that registered distance is the only factor determining size. One of us (I.R.) has sought to demonstrate the importance of an entirely different factor in size perception and size constancy. See I. Rock and S. Ebenholtz, *Psychological Review*, 1959, 66, 387.

[5] The failure to obtain a substantial illusion with slides does not contradict this conclusion, because other distance correlates seem to operate in the direction of revealing the slide's two-dimensionality.

one hand the horizon moon can be said to take on the size of a region of the terrain of equivalent visual angle at the horizon. That region, in turn, has a large phenomenal size because of the constancy function—the observer's tendency to take distance into account. (This way of stating the matter is similar but not identical to the popular explanation that the horizon moon looks large because we compare it with familiar objects seen adjacent to it on the horizon. For example, the image of the moon is larger than that of a house on the horizon. Ergo, the moon is at least larger than a house. The fact is, however, that familiar objects need not be present, as in the case of the moon seen over the ocean. But one *can* say that the moon must be at least as large as an extent of water of equivalent visual angle at the horizon, and that that extent is seen to be quite large because of the constancy function. See **Figure 4.**)

By contrast, the zenith moon cannot be related to any other regions of the field, and in that sense its distance is essentially indeterminate. In fact, it is more or less a reduction object. We have shown that the horizon moon viewed through an aperture appears to be the same size as the zenith moon. Although the distance of the zenith moon is indeterminate, relative to the horizon moon the zenith moon nevertheless seems to register as "nearer."

If this way of putting the matter is correct, it suggests an interesting explanation of the error of the standard, discussed earlier. When the observer views the horizon moon as the standard he approaches the zenith variable with the immediate memory of a disk which, at least to some extent, is seen as a thing with an objective size (if not a thing of any *particular* linear size). When, however, the zenith moon is the standard, because his viewing of it is more of a "pure visual angle" of "pure extensity" experience, he approaches the horizon variable with a visual-angle set. It is known that such a set can reduce the tendency toward constancy (Gilinsky, 1955). In the instance under discussion, it would reduce the illusion when the zenith moon is the standard. According to this interpretation, the error we obtained may be viewed as a special case and not as an instance of a more general error of the standard, as was implied earlier.

This leads to a second reason for stating that the apparent-distance hypothesis is oversimplified. As noted earlier the zenith

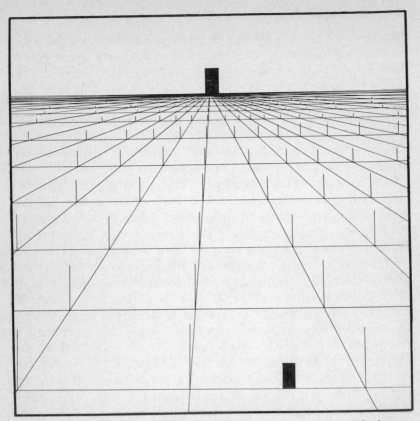

FIGURE 4. The effect of distance on size. The black rectangle on the horizon appears larger than the one in the foreground, although they are identical in size. The effect would be much greater in viewing a truly three-dimensional scene, where binocular and other cues would enhance the impression of depth. Conversely, the effect can be increased by viewing the picture with only one eye, because the impression of the two-dimensional surface of the page can be somewhat reduced.

moon is at an indeterminate distance and is therefore of indeterminate size. The horizon moon appears very far away, and objects at very great distances also are of somewhat indeterminate size.[6]

[6] If the size of the zenith moon is indeterminate and that of the horizon moon is quasi-determinate, one might argue that it should be as difficult to compare the two moons directly as it is to compare either with a nearby object (Boring's method). This is not the case, however, because the horizon moon, being so very distant, is not perceived as of a definite linear size and is perceived, therefore, as more or less commensurate with the zenith moon.

Ordinarily we say that distance is taken into account in a particular impression of linear size; thus, as stated in Emmert's law, a greater distance yields an impression of a particular larger size. In the case of the moon illusion we have to extend this reasoning to say that distance influences size perception (in the sense that one moon looks larger than the other) despite the fact that neither moon appears to be of any specifiable size. That is, in the case of the moon illusion it would seem that distance affects the relative-extensity experience, not a relative-linear-size experience.

MISCELLANEOUS CONSIDERATIONS. The moon illusion has often been cited as an example of the anisotropy of visual space, in that there is a nonequivalence of phenomenal space in different directions. In our opinion, not only is this term not clear but it presupposes something which may not be true. *Anisotropy* could refer to direction within two-dimensional space—could pertain to facts such as the phenomenal changes and recognition changes brought about by disorientation of shapes (for example, a square becomes a diamond when tilted 45°, or text is difficult to read upside down). Or it could refer to three-dimensional space. In either case it remains to be proved that phenomenal changes such as those just mentioned, or the moon illusion (or the presumably related fact that size constancy is more marked in the horizontal than in the vertical direction), require an explanation in which visual space is, per se, anisotropic. The two-dimensional effects can perhaps be explained in a different fashion (Rock, 1956; Rock and Heimer, 1957)), and the apparent-distance explanation of the moon illusion is based on the different *content* of the visual scene in the different directions. Our failure to achieve anything more than a minute effect in the dark-field experiments argues against any inherent anisotropy of three-dimensional space.

The question of whether the moon illusion is based on an experiential enlargement of the horizon moon or a shrinkage of the zenith moon has often been raised. Such a question presupposes a normative base line against which the effect can be measured. In the Müller-Lyer illusion one might compare either line seen within the arrowheads with one seen in isolation and ask, Is the illusion due to the apparent enlargement of the line seen within the outward-pointing arrowheads, to the apparent diminution of the line seen within the inward-pointing arrowheads, or possibly to both? Here the isolated line is the base line, and the question can be investigated. In the case of the moon illusion, however, there is no "normal"-size moon, and the visual angle remains constant. From the standpoint of the tendency toward size constancy, however, one might say that the horizon moon approaches the veridical size of the moon more closely than the zenith moon does. Of course, the departure from constancy is extremely large in either case, but it is somewhat less for the horizon moon. Therefore, if the illusion is defined in terms of size constancy (or the objectively true size of the moon), one must conclude that it is based on the smaller appearance of the zenith moon resulting from the inadequate registration of distance, which was discussed earlier.

As is evident from Table 1 of part 1 (Kaufman and Rock, 1962) and from the variability reported for many of the experiments, there are great differences in the illusion for different individuals; this was true in all experiments where an average illusion of any magnitude was found. Findings for individual observers were consistent in repetitions of the experiment ($r = .82$ for the experiment on the effect of distance and cloud condition) and even from condition to condition ($r = .83$ for the experiment on the effect of eye elevation). How should we interpret such consistent individual differences? It is possible to argue that some observers respond more readily than others on the basis of visual angle uninfluenced, so to speak, by distance. Thus, in the literature on size constancy it has often been argued that there are "analytical" perceivers who show less than average tendency toward constancy (Thouless, 1932). Such persons presumably would not experience much of a moon illusion. Although this may indeed be the case, we are somewhat reluctant to accept the notion that the actual sensory experience of the moon's size differs for different individuals viewing the moon at the same time and in the same place. The alternative is the somewhat radical proposition that, while perceived size does not vary, the judgments nevertheless do vary because the comparison is a more difficult one to make than would be the case if two disks were simultaneously perceived on the same background at the same distance. Faced with the difficulty of making a precise match—where it is necessary for the observer to remember the size of the standard while he inspects the variable series—each observer settles on a particular value and then, in order to be consistent, continues to select a value close to his original choice. Of course, such variability centers around a value which reflects the illusion per se. It is possible that a nonperceptual process of this kind accounts for individual differences in various perceptual tasks reported in the psychological literature.

SUMMARY AND CONCLUSIONS

We have examined the two types of explanations of the moon illusion—the egocentric, in which the differences in direction of the horizon and the zenith moons are thought of in relation to different angles of regard of the observer, and the objective, in which the presence or absence of the terrain is considered crucial. The former type is exemplified chiefly by the eye-elevation hypothesis in the work of Boring and his colleagues; the latter, by the apparent-distance hypothesis based on the superior cues to distance provided by the terrain. Boring had rejected the apparent-distance hypothesis on the grounds that the horizon moon is reported as nearer, not farther away, by most observers. He then performed experiments which supported the eye-elevation hypothesis.

Our own work started with our reservations about Boring's conclusions because of (1) logical considerations and contradictory data of our own concerning the question of which moon appears to be farther away; (2) the observation that in daily life eye-elevation does not seem to account for the moon illusion; and (3) logical difficulties connected with Boring's method of studying the phenomenal size of the moon. We developed an apparatus which made it possible for an observer to view an artificial moon in the sky at optical infinity. The size of this moon could then be varied. Using two such units, one pointed at the horizon and one at the zenith, the observer could compare the moons directly with one another and match the variable with the standard. A series of experiments were performed with this apparatus. The major conclusions from these experiments are as follows.

1) An appreciable illusion is obtained, varying in average magnitude from a diameter ratio of 1.2 to a ratio of 1.6, depending on terrain and sky conditions.

2) Eye-elevation does not account for the moon illusion (nor, for that matter, does head elevation).

3) A minute illusion (ratio 1.03) is obtained in a completely dark field for binocularly viewed moons at optical infinity. The reliability and possible significance of this slight effect warrant further study, but it is clear that whatever produces the effect cannot be considered a factor of any importance in the ordinary moon illusion.

4) Neither apparent color nor brightness can even partially account for the moon illusion. The frequently noted reddish color of the horizon moon, or its lower brightness as compared with the brightness of the zenith moon, or both, are apparently coincidental concomitants of the phenomenal size.

5) The presence of the terrain is crucial for the existence of the illusion. The evidence is as follows: (a) The illusion disappears when the observer's view of the terrain is obstructed; (b) the illusion can be obtained when a reduction horizon moon (here analogous to a zenith moon) is compared with a normally viewed horizon moon; and (c) the illusion can be reversed with respect to the direction of regard by means of mirrors, so that the elevated moon seen directly above the terrain's "horizon" looks larger.

6) The apparent (or better, the registered) distance along the terrain plays a causal role. The evidence is as follows: (a) The illusion is considerably reduced when the terrain is optically inverted; (b) the illusion can be shown to be a function of the apparent distance to the horizon and of the degree of cloudiness; and (c) only a minute illusion can be produced indoors by means of slides that yield an impression of a terrain, although the patterns of the slides are structurally similar to outdoor patterns which do yield an illusion. The only difference would seem to be that the slides do not convey a sufficient impression of depth. No illusion at all is produced by control slides which duplicate the structural features of terrain but which do not yield an impression of depth.

7) There is some evidence that a secondary factor contributes to the moon illusion under certain special conditions—namely, a framing or relational effect when the horizon moon is seen between buildings or other large terrestrial objects.

8) The illusion is greater when the horizon moon is the standard than when the zenith moon is the standard, a fact which may be an

instance of what has recently come to be known as the error of the standard.

9) The apparent-distance hypothesis as an explanation of the moon illusion requires some elaboration. (a) Distance influences the apparent size of the moon despite the fact that the moon does not appear to be of any specifiable linear size (distance here affects the relative-extensity experience, not the linear-size experience). (b) The zenith moon, while appearing less far away than the horizon moon, is to some extent a reduction object—its distance is essentially indeterminate. (c) The observer may not be consciously aware that he is responding to a greater subjectively registered distance in viewing the horizon moon. In fact, when asked to compare the distances of the two moons, he may even judge the horizon moon to be the nearer. The latter judgment, however, depends strictly upon the relative sizes of the two moons.

[7]
Machines Cannot Fight Alone [1]

S. S. STEVENS

According the naval lieutenant everybody was unhinged by the end of that day. When the battle is on and the give-and-take is of rugged proportions you expect casualties, but on a beautiful day in the South Pacific with nothing but friends for 300 miles around the loss of one of the boys does something to you. It leaves you too numb to talk and it haunts you in your bunk. The lieutenant was

---

[1] Much of the research referred to in this article was carried out by various laboratories operating under contract with the Office of Scientific Research and Development. Research on some of the psychophysical problems discussed is continuing at the Psycho-Acoustic Laboratory, Harvard University, under contract with the U. S. Navy Office of Research and Inventions.

SOURCE: S. S. Stevens, "Machines Cannot Fight Alone," *American Scientist*, July 1946, 3, 389–400. Reprinted by permission of the *American Scientist* and S. S. Stevens.

Intercept Officer on the carrier and throughout the whole ordeal he stood watch in the nerve center of the ship—where all the "dope" from the radios and radars is pooled and weighed and acted upon. The nerves of the ship were frayed at their ends on that August day.

By 1400 hours the patrol plane was overdue. At 1410 the pilot cut in with his radio requesting "homing." He couldn't find the carrier. The officer known as the FDO took over and told him to stand by while they got a radar "fix" on him. The pilot had to ask a repeat on this "Static bad out here," he said. Later it cleared up a little and conversation went back and forth while the radar operator scanned his screen for the tell-tale "pip" of the patrol plane. But in three of its sectors the radar screen was cluttered with interference and the operator got tense as he twisted his knobs and strained his eyes for the tiny pip that would locate the plane. "Radar can't see you yet, thunderstorms around," called the FDO. "Thunderstorms north of here," answered the pilot, "static getting worse again."

Time dragged on and all other business gradually stopped while everybody waited and watched. The room got quieter. At 1430 the radar operator, with the help of some kibitzers who had gathered around to lend an eye, came up with a fix near the edge of a patch of clutter. The plane seemed to be emerging from the area of a thunderstorm—on the far side from the carrier. The FDO grabbed the microphone. "You are 30 miles from the ship. Steer 357."

"Say again," from the pilot.

"You are south of the ship," shouted the FDO a little desperately.

"Static terrible, can just tell you are talking," came the answer.

"Steer 357. I say again, steer 357" loudly and firmly pronounced the FDO.

"Gasoline low," called the pilot, "not hearing you any more. Are you hearing me?"

They were hearing him, but not too well; static was all over the place. The FDO kept calling. In supreme frustration he talked every way he knew how; loudly, softly, imploringly, profanely. And he kept at it for a full half hour after the Status Board showed that no gasoline could possibly be left in the tanks of the patrol plane.

That evening at the wardroom mess the Executive Officer was heard to damn the business of trusting men's lives to radars a man can't see and to radios he can't hear.

The "Exec" was both right and wrong. He was really directing a complaint at the human side of engineering, at the art of gearing machines to the minds and muscles of men, in short, at the science known as psychophysics. He was asking that the gadgets of war be dominated by men, in the sense that man is the master of the gasoline buggy—where his dominion is so sure that he even allows woman to drive. But just as the automobile evolved from a contrary contraption ill fitting its operator, so must the devices of battle grow from crudity to a harmonious integration with the soldier. It takes time. And in the kind of war just concluded, where feverish development heaped complication on complication, the struggles of human engineering were valiant, if not always triumphant.

THE SCIENCE OF HUMAN SENSES

This recent war was different from other wars in the peculiar respect that it was fought largely on margin—sensory margin— where the battle hangs on the power of the eyes or the ears to make a fine discrimination, to estimate a distance, to see or hear a signal which is just at the edge of human capacity. Radars don't see, radios don't hear, sonars don't detect, guns don't point without someone making a fine sensory judgment, and the paradox of it is that the faster the engineers and the inventors served up their "automatic" gadgets to eliminate the human factor the tighter the squeeze became on the powers of the operator—the man who must see and hear and judge and act with that margin of superiority which gives his outfit the jump on the enemy.

When a new device in the field fell short of the miracle it could so obviously perform in the laboratory, the engineers despaired and blamed it on poor training, deliberate misuse, or some combination of the two. Some of the laboratories got wiser and sent a scientist along with the "gismo" to prove that its virtues were really those alleged in the first paragraph of the instruction manual. It helped. But the boys out front still liked to wail about those people who design electromechanical marvels to be operated by a man with three arms and an ability to see around a corner in pitch darkness. What was needed, of course, was a knowledge of man's capacities, his powers of discrimination and the factors which affect them. The machine had to be built for *Homo sapiens* to operate. When it was he used it, and given a new leverage on the situation he promptly pushed his flights and his missiles and his electromagnetic beams out farther until he was again at the ragged edge of his sensory endowments, where he was left chafing anew at the dumb insentience of knobs and dials and gears and coils, stolid and stubborn in their indifference to serving a human will.

So psychophysics found itself at war, hesitant at first, bewildered by sudden practical demands, but confident that its hand should be in wherever the human senses set the problem. Broadly defined, psychophysics is the science of the senses in action. And since a soldier cannot even pull an effective trigger without an elaborate integration of sensory data from his eyes and muscles, the devotees of this science found themselves poking about in almost every corner of the military structure. Their tools are basically those of G. T. Fechner, physicist and philosopher, who in 1860 gave us a treatise on the facts and procedures of a new science of the "relation between mind and matter"—meaning the relation between sensation and the stimulus that causes it.

The new science soon shed its founder's preoccupation with metaphical issues and grew up to become an indispensable part of psychology and human engineering. The methods outlined by Fechner have been extended and put to use (sometimes unwittingly, perhaps) by physicists, radio engineers, airplane designers, training officers, psychologists—in fact by all whose business it is to adapt machines to men and to get the best out of men by way of technical performance in an age of technological profusion. Whatever the task or the skill required, whatever the human sense employed, there are rules governing the actions and discriminations of men which make one way of doing things better than another. These are the rules of psychophysics.

How the old rules were dug up and dusted off and new rules were discovered for solving new problems created by new devices is the human story of our machine-age war. Implicit in the tale is the brief that the nature of man still determines the shape of his world, and of his wars, and that the science of man and his capacities must run hand in hand with technology if simple effective harmony is to ensue.

EYES AND THE RADAR SCREEN

Perhaps nothing in World War II was so dramatically transformed into an efficient weapon as was radar. The atomic bomb stole the scene at the final curtain, but nuclear fission did not fight the war—it only ended it. With radar it was a continuous frantic race to throw a better and better radio beam farther and farther out, and to get back a reflection which could be displayed as a meaningful pattern before the eyes of an operator. Now the returning echo of a radar beam, detected and transformed into a pattern on the screen of a cathode-ray oscilloscope, is not a very meaningful sight to the unskilled eye. On an A-scope we see, when conditions are good, a bright horizontal line with a pip or spike projecting from it. The pip is the echo we are looking for and its position along the horizontal line tells us how far it is from us to the target. When conditions are not so good—which has a way of being whenever it really matters—we see a horizontal sweep of dancing, wiggling pips known to the art as "grass" and one of the tiny blades is the pip we are looking for. It is a search for one particular straw in a haymow.

Actually, radar quickly progressed to the point at which a good operator could easily pick out the pip for an enemy plane or ship at moderate distances when conditions were reasonably normal, but the interesting thing about the race between the ingenuity of the inventors and the level of aspiration of the armed services is that the best in equipment is never quite good enough. If an enemy vessel can be detected at 50 miles on a good day the submarine commander wants to push the radar to detect a sampan at 100 miles in a thunderstorm—because that is where you sometimes find the sampan. Despite the understandable complaints of the designers that their gear was never intended for this or for that, its use often got stretched right up to the point where the sensory powers of the operators became the factor of limitation. "Pipology" became psychophysics.

But even without this enthusiasm to make a good instrument do a better job, there was still the enemy to contend with. If nature did not grow grass on the scopes the enemy sometimes did. He had ways of jamming radar by sending out interference which made it look as though the world were a solid mass of targets. And in the face of this interference the operator had to use every available cue, no matter how ephemeral, to aid his sensory judgment in the correct identification of the meaningful pips.

PSYCHOPHYSICS IN RADAR ENGINEERING

Real progress in the task of squeezing these last precious increments in efficiency from the radar equipment and from the operators came through the application of psychophysical procedures. It was found that a man's ability to "read" a scope under adverse circumstances is governed by a host of factors. His skill depends upon the size of the screen, the length of the pip, the rate at which the radar pulses succeed one another, the color of the image on the screen, the brightness of the light in the radar room, etc. Each factor can be isolated in the laboratory, and by controlled psychophysical tests the optical viewing conditions can be discovered. It was even possible to work out standards to be met by the manufacturers of radar screens which would ensure a product engineered to the requirements of the human eye.

With other types of radars using other tricks, such as the PPI-scope which paints for the operator a complete map of the territory about him, the problem is not really different—only varied in its complications. When a PPI presentation is at its best it is nothing short of miraculous. From high in the air, through a matted carpet of thick clouds, the City of New York may show up in such detail that one can see at which of the piers along the river ships are berthed and whether or not the traffic is heavy in Central Park. Mostly, however, the PPI presentation is a fuzzy pattern of cloud-like formations with isolated wisps which the adroit "pipologist" may interpret as airplanes, ships, islands or cities, depending on very subtle cues indeed. If there is consistent evidence that the wisp has moved it is probably a plane. If the brightness of the pip grows and fades in a certain systematic fashion it may be deduced that the plane is flying at a particular altitude. From such tenuous cues as the height and width of a menacing pip the FDO on an aircraft carrier might judge the strength of the enemy flight and decide upon the number of fighters required to block the attack. Mistakes mean lives.

Here again the problem of human abilities is obviously para-mount, and a long list of factors has been shown to color the work-manship of the operators. Sometimes improvement in radar has come from deliberate and sometimes from casual psychophysical studies. Sometimes it has been trial and error exclusively, sometimes engineering shrewdness, sometimes luck—both good and bad. And there have ben some dramatic failures.

Still under official wraps is the story of a device intended to transpose the picture on the PPI directly to a large circular map-like surface on which the operator could draw lines, make measurements and keep records of movements. The idea was brimming with prom-ise, the engineering was superb, models were completed and sent to the fleet. Soon the reports of the commanders began seeping back to Washington. Verdict: washout.

The plain fact of the matter now seems to be that this handsome gadget succeeded in all respects save that of satisfying the demands imposed by the way in which nature created man. The picture was there, but men could see it only partly and uncertainly. The simple factors of visual contrast, size, illumination and arrangement—factors which make or break the power of sensory discriminations—did not combine to give the operator the advantage that had been so confidently expected. So back to the laboratory again, this time for some psychophysics. An analysis of the performance of a group of trained operators soon showed up the more obvious reasons for the dissatisfaction of the task forces, and a program of correction and redesign was instituted. The end of this particular story is still in the offing.

The business of jamming radars by sending out interference to clutter up the enemy's radar screens was an art at which we excelled the Germans and the Japs. We had to be better at it, because we were taking the fight to the enemy by flying straight above his home grounds. He used his radars to aim his antiaircraft guns, and when left unmolested his accuracy was far too great for our comfort. We had two main tricks in our bag: we could scatter tinfoil about the sky to make it seem to the enemy operators that the air was full of targets and cause him to shoot at the plane that wasn't there, or we could broadcast random, "noisy" radar beams from our own transmitters which would blanket his scopes with grass and pips, and leave him no room to see through to the real target. Both methods had their psychological aspects, but it was especially the procedure of jamming by radiated interference that was brought to full effectiveness by a team of psychologists and engineers working together on the problem of what the eyes can see. A large new laboratory and millions of dollars were devoted to fouling the eyes of the enemy, and the ultimate specification of the best means for throwing interference at him stemmed in large measure from the psychophysical tests. Preconceptions of radio engineers were altered, development projects were stopped or changed or started, tactical doctrine was rewritten, all because of what a few human guinea pigs could or could not perceive when different kinds of radio signals were beamed at the radars they were trying to operate.

INSIGNIA FOR EYES TO SEE

Not infrequently some of the most important contributions of pschophysics are so simple and are brought forth so casually that the whole procedure seems to be merely the application of a little common sense. When the Japs came winging in over Pearl Harbor our airplanes bore as their identifying markings the proud insignia of a blue circle enclosing a white star. This circular pattern is a pretty thing when viewed from a middle distance, but seen from far off it degenerates, unhappily, into a simple round spot devoid of distinctiveness. The Japs also wore spots on their wings. The color was different, to be sure, but to an excited gunner a spot is a spot, or rather a speck is a speck, and it is reported (with unknown reliability) that some gunners held their fire from the enemy, and · some let go at their friends. In the European theatre the British were using circles too. The Germans had designed themselves a fairly legible cross, so that the problem for the British was not too acute, except that the likeness of the British and American insignia made confusion. Something had to be done, for our own bullets piercing the bodies of our friends was too terrible a price for the failure of a sensory discrimination. A device different from a circle and unlike a German cross was called for.

A variety of posisble designs were prepared on placards and these were shown to groups of people under various conditions and at assorted distances in order to discover which emblem was optimally distinctive and identifiable. Choice lay with the now familiar circle, star and bar. This approach to the problem was common sense at its scientific best.

Fighting in the Dark

The few to whom so many owed so much in 1940 had a very special problem of their own. It was a problem as old as the art of warfare, but in the second phase of the Battle of Britain it was given new urgency by the fact that men were zooming through the skies in the dark of night, where the eyes of a cat would have been something less than adequate. The GI in a jungle foxhole needs night vision to spot the slinking foe, the sailor on lookout duty needs it even more perhaps, for on the power of his eyes to pierce the darkness may rest the safety of the ship. But with the night fighter in a speeding plane, hunting the sky for the enemy bomber, a low visual threshold is absolutely imperative. The problem was so serious that numerous research groups both here and abroad were recruited to the cause of finding solutions.

These solutions lay in several directions, some built on new knowledge, some involving better use of old wisdom. The ancient and obvious fact that some men see better in the dark than do others led directly to the development of new and more reliable methods for sorting aviators in order to put a finger on the dangerous cases of partial night blindness. The newer discoveries of the factors affecting night vision, such as its relation to vitamin A, were brought to bear as an adjunct to training programs. So exhaustive were some of the psychophysical studies that even such a minor matter as the shine on the pilot's nose was shown to be measurable in its influence on his ability to pick out a darkened target. Equally careful studies of the temporal course of dark adaptation (the speed with which our night vision improves as we remain in the dark) brought changes in the routine of briefing and take-off, and in the kinds of lighting used in the cockpit.

It takes about half an hour for the eyes to become completely accustomed to very dim illumination. That is why we fumble our way along theater aisles when we first enter from the bright outdoors but find it quite easy to negotiate the return trip. For the pilot sweating out his call to the ready-room it is clumsy and distressing to preserve his dark adaptation by avoiding all lighted places. Nevertheless, if he is not maximally prepared for seeing in the dark his mission might as well end while he is still safely on the bench. Most of the frustration of slowly adapting eyes was finally circumvented by what is perhaps the smartest invention in this area of psychophysics. It is simplicity itself. All the pilot has to do is wear special red goggles during the half hour before take-off. Then, when he lifts the goggles he is almost 100-percent dark adapted and ready to fly by the light of the stars. This simple dodge is possible because different elements in the retina of the eye are sensitive to different kinds of light, so that we can use the "cones" at the center of the retina to see in red light while the red-blind "rods" surrounding the cones are protected from the colors which stimulate them. Since their kind of light does not get past the red goggles, the rods can ignore what the cones are doing and proceed to get themselves ready to respond to feeble illuminants. Actually it is the rods that are most sensitive to faint light, and they have their greatest sensitivity to blues and greens.

The red goggles do not solve all the pilot's problems, however. Unfortunately, the sensitive rods are not located in the center of the retina (the fovea) on which the image falls when we look straight at a small object. They cover the region all around the fovea, and they are stimulated by the objects we see out of the corner of the eye. Naturally, therefore, when the night fighter looks directly at a distant plane so that its image falls on the center of his retina he is unable to see it. If he looks away the plane reappears, only to attract his attention and vanish again when he looks at it. This hide-and-seek can be stopped by drumming into the pilot, through training and practice, a skill at paying attention to things in the outskirts of the visual field and suppressing the natural tendency to watch only what happens at the center. It is amazing how skillfully a man can learn to aim a gun without ever looking directly at the target.

MUSCLES AND SKILLS

Sometimes an obvious improvement is no improvement at all. The stresses on a modern warrior are multiple and complex, but so are the requirements of his job. Often he must suffer vexation of one sort for advantages of another. He must compromise.

Early in the war when certain psychophysical laboratories were probing the causes of pilot fatigue in an effort to discover the reason for frequent crack-ups in landing, attention centered itself on the problem of vibration. It was reasoned that a man subjected to an unnatural jiggling for hours on end might well be the worse for it. Direct proof of the evils of vibration was not at hand, but since any good guess was a good gamble, a project was launched to produce a vibrationless seat. Modes of vibration in aircraft were studied, compliances were analyzed, and suspensions were tested. Finally, a seat was produced which floated in rubber so completely that little of the normal agitation of the plane could be passed on to the pilot's anatomy. It was dispatched to the Navy for test, and several pilots gave it a try. They were full of compliments for the scientists who had so cleverly subdued the vibration, but they did not like the seat. Not that it wasn't more comfortable, but it gave them an eerie sensation of being somewhat remote from the plane. They wanted to fly by the seat of their pants and feel the plane, with all its strainings and motions, solidly beneath them. They would rather be shaken than float.

The sensations from our muscles belong to what is known as the kinaesthetic sense. It is the sense which tell us in what position we have left our hands and feet without our having to look at them to see. All problems involving normal skills and coordination are founded on kinaesthesis, and when the airplane pilot pulls on his controls and the gunner cranks in his gun-laying data they operate on the basis of this sense. For most military skills there is a right and wrong arrangement of the levers and handles that are given the soldier to manage. The stick and rudder bar of a plane can be too stiff or too easy to move in relation to their effect on the behavior of the plane. If the controls are too sensitive the ship is said to be "hot" and it is sometimes a serious matter for the cadet to learn to tone down his muscular adjustments as he graduates from trainers to highspeed fighter planes. If the stick is made too stiff and the response of the plane too sluggish in relation to the pilot's muscle sense, he is apt to come off second best in his next dog fight. Likewise, in tracking a moving target by turning the cranks which aim and point the muzzle, a gunner finds that there is an optimal size of wheel, stiffness of rotation, and speed of cranking for greatest accuracy.

This topic of muscular skills and the rules of the game they play is far too little understood by the engineers, and by the psychophysicists themselves. Interesting research has been carried out during the war and more is promised for the future. But the problem is complicated, just as the human being is complicated, and if machines are to be the servants of men there can be no letup in this human side of engineering.

PASSING THE WORD

It has been said that this recent world conflict was a war of communications. So were most other wars. Drama packs the history of messages received in the nick of time, of messages delayed or lost or intercepted, but for the real story of communication in World War II we must look to the everyday business of "passing the word." In those massive operations calling for the coordination of ships and planes and tanks and guns and all their multiplicity of gimmicks and gismoes, everything moves on the split second, and the nerves which flex the muscles of the warring giants are telephone lines and radio beams—with men at both ends of the circuit. Wig-wag, searchlight blinkers and telegraphy still have their uses, but they are slow. The pace calls for speech—snappy messages, curtly spoken and immediately understood. The waist gunner with a new "bandit" looming in his gun-sight has no time to code his message to the rest of the crew in dots and dashes. "Tally-ho, three o'clock," fills his quota of seconds. Then it is chatter, chatter, bang, and the tail-gunner takes the bandit over as he sails away in the direction of "seven o'clock." Even speech was often too slow when the *kamikaze* came boring in and the radar lookout had to relay his data on the "contact" through the ship's information center to the gun directors. On too many of our ships the tearing boom of a suicide strike preceded the bark of the gun that should have dropped the attacker into the sea.

As in many other quests for better harmony between the operators and their gadgets, the methods of psychophysics were turned to account in two different ways: men were trained in the best use of existing equipment, and new devices were developed. Nursed by the urgency of these problems, there grew up and flourished a special area psychophysics, called *psycho-acoustics*, complete with laboratories and field stations. The claim can be made that the net improvement in certain vital communications added up to anywhere from 50 to several hundred percent.

The communication system that is accepted as the ideal or standard system is also the simplest: it is merely the air itself. Two people a yard apart in a quiet room and talking to each other in conversational tones find themselves on either end of the world's best communication link. It is nature's own device. We dignify it by the impressive title, *orthotelephonic circuit*, and we set its performance up as something for all other systems to shoot at. The listener on nature's circuit hears practically 100 percent of all clearly spoken words, and this percentage is called the *articulation score* of the system. The articulation scores for other systems usually range below 100 per cent, especially under the stresses and strains of combat conditions.

When the talker is wearing an oxygen mask and gasping for breath at 30,000 feet, and the listener is curled up half frozen in a belly turret with the noise of the propellers pounding in his ears, it is remarkable that any messages get across. To a tired and nervous crew a pilot once yelled, "Hand me a bottle, my oxygen line is leaking." The waist gunners bailed out convinced that the skipper had ordered, "Cutting the throttle, clear out for a crash landing."

It was easy to improve upon the gear we were using in 1941 because it was already obsolescent. The lethargy of peace in the pause between the wars! The earphones that our aviators first took into combat were of the vintage 1923. The earphone cushions allowed the noise of the plane to leak through and interfere with what the listener was trying to hear. No microphone suitable for use in an oxygen mask was even in existence, and the pinch-hitting throat microphone was, and is, a hopeless device intended to pluck speech off the Adam's apple where only a wubbly, hot-potato kind of sound is produced. All in all, our interphone systems were caught with their vowels down, while at the same time engineers were bringing up new airplanes, bigger, faster, more powerful—and noisier. *Say again* was a very common phrase in those days.

Some planes and tanks and landing vehicles are so noisy that a man can scarcely understand a person shouting directly in his ear. The noise crowds up tight against the ceiling of the ear's ability to respond leaving no room for speech sounds, no matter how amplified, to squeeze in. Here the problem is twofold: to seal the ear against the noise by a well-designed cushion around the earphone and to shield the microphone so that it does not pick up the noise and pass it on to the listener. The neatest trick in this line was the development of a "noise-canceling" microphone, so designed that the noise gets at the diaphragm from two directions and cancels itself out. Hanging just in front of the lips, it takes in the speech sounds from only one direction, without canceling.

If with these devices the ear is still overloaded by noise the psychophysicist is ready with another recommendation: put plugs in the ears. Strangely enough, speech is better heard in a noisy place if the ears are tightly plugged, preferably with the scientific little neoprene stoppers engineered for the Army and Navy, but if not, then with cotton or even with the fingers. Try it sometime.

The voice also comes in for its troubles. Ask the man who has tried to sound clear and precise from inside a gas mask, or an oxygen mask, or a diving suit. The back pressure on the voice seems to take the starch out of the vowels and consonants, leaving them limp and mushy. In addition there is the effect of altitude itself. When we fill our lungs at 35,000 feet we take in only one fourth the number of molecules inhaled at sea level, and only one fourth the normal mass of air is available to drive the vocal cords. So the aviator huffs and puffs, and blows practically nothing at all. He speaks in short gasps and sounds like a man at the end of a marathon. The quality of the voice also changes in complicated ways, and as yet no scientific cunning has succeeded in making sub-stratosphere speech sound entirely natural.

PACKAGING SPEECH

Other triumphs have rewarded the researcher, however.

The scientist is particularly pleased with himself when he contrives to improve upon nature. If in the process he is able to fly into the face of accepted dogma and turn up with a wrinkle which proves that what was "obvious" is really wrong he rubs his hands and tingles with the thrill of discovery. At the start of the war the dogma inhibiting progress in radio transmission was the obvious notion that any distortion in the sounds of speech is bad, that speech after nature's pattern is most intelligible to the ear. This notion is sound enough in the normal instance where the transmission system is not beset on the one hand by limitations of power, and on the other by the military urgency to make the radio serve its function over the longest possible span. But for projecting the voice over the greatest distance with the least radio power, normal, natural, undistorted speech is less effective than speech that has been chopped down and distorted and squeezed into an efficient package.

Psycho-acoustic studies on the intelligibility of radio transmission disclosed that the rule for packaging speech is to snip the tops off the large speech waves and amplify the small ones. The large waves are the vowel sounds, and they are easy to understand in spite of severe distortion. The small waves are the consonants. They are the critical sounds that enable us to tell *tape* from *take* from *bake* from *shape* from *shake*. They are the sounds that must be carefully preserved and amplified in transmission.

Applied to the design of radio transmitters the process of clipping the peaks of speech brought new standards of performance to military radio and new conceptions as to the distance to be covered by a given strength of beam. Obviously, the procedure is no good for commercial broadcasts where listener appeal is the product for sale, but the boy whose life depends on a clear message will happily forego the charm of rounded vowels and liquid tones in order to understand correctly. Forty percent distortion from clipping is not sweet to the ear, but with amounts as great as this it has been possible to stretch the usable length of the radio beam to double its normal range.

All this was the result of tailoring speech and radio procedures to the requirements of the human ear. Out of four years of such testing, studying, designing, and retesting, during which more than two million test words were spoken to crews of listeners over radio and telephone systems under all varieties of storm and stress, there has come a total revision of the basic components of aircraft interphones. We fought the last battles of the war with new earphones, new microphones, new helmets, new amplifiers, new oxygen masks, all of them engineered in the light of the all-important human factor.

THE FUTURE

As with the aircraft interphone, so with almost every other fighting tool. Throughout the entire war, in each campaign and skirmish, on every ship and plane, in all the earth-bound foxholes and at every GHQ men strained at their machines. Wherever men stared searching into the darkness or taxed their eyes at a radar screen, wherever they held their breath to hear the tell-tale echo from the enemy under the sea or twisted their knobs and dials to launch destruction at the foe, the psychophysicist went along in spirit, fretting about the eyes and ears and muscles of the men and scheming to devise a greater harmony between the soldier and his tools. The laboratories were hives of workers beating their brains for new ideas. The factories purred with the whir of creation and gorged the arsenal with new implements of war. In the final drive to victory there were few important weapons used that bore exact resemblance to the gear employed when we first were jarred from slumber by the rudeness of aggression.

It is a proud story, perhaps, but something of a scandal too. It depends on how you want to look at it. However it is judged, we are left at this moment face up against decision. Are we now going to send the psychophysicists and all their scientific colleagues back to their universities and their peace-time desks and leave our armed forces to enter the next war with the droppings of the last one? Then are we going to rush the scientists back to the frantic task of designing new gadgets and fitting them to human capabilities when the enemy is already upon is? Or are we going to keep science and human engineering alive with encouragement and support, holding one eye on the aspiration to make life more livable while we inhabit our spot of earth, and the other on the business of ensuring that no one takes it from us?

[8]
Relations Between the Central Nervous System and the Peripheral Organs

E. VON HOLST

   The relation of the Central Nervous System (CNS) to the peripheral senses and muscular movement is an old and much discussed problem. Here we are at the heart of the physiology of behaviour, and in comparison to that which is not known, our present knowledge is very meagre and vague! Under these circumstances, our knowledge and conceptions are dependent upon the method which happens to be popular at the moment. In this field, the method which has played the greatest role consists of, first, artificially inactivating the CNS and then, through peripheral stimulation, evoking a particular response. On this basis, the CNS is often held to be only a reflex-machanism, yet we know today that this view is onesided. In order to be in co-ordinated activity, the CNS often needs a minimum of stimulation or loading by afferent impulses; the conception of chain-reflex co-ordination has been recognised almost everywhere as being incorrect. Isolated, that is de-afferented, parts

   SOURCE: E. von Holst, "Relations Between the Central Nervous System and the Peripheral Organs," *Animal Behaviour*, 1954, 2, 89–94. Reprinted by permission of Bailliére, Tindall & Cox Ltd.

of the nervous system show continued electrical activity. One can therefore say that, as a rule, de-afferented ganglion cells, under otherwise normal conditions, possess "automaticity."

These facts allow us to regard the function of the peripheral senses from a new viewpoint. The classical reflex-concept assumes that the peripheral stimulus initiates the central nervous activity. Since we now know that this supposed cause is often unnecessary, it is possible to start from the CNS. We can ask the question, what effect is produced on the sensory-receptors by the motor impulses which initiate a muscular movement? Thus, we look from the opposite direction, not from the outside inward, but from the centre to periphery. You will quickly see that in this manner we shall come upon new problems and experimentally verifiable hypotheses.

In order to make myself clear, I should like first to explain a few terms. The whole of the impulses which are produced by whatever stimuli in whatever receptors I shall term *afference,* and in contradistinction to this I shall call the whole of the motor impulses *efference.* Efference can only be present when ganglion cells are active; afference, on the contrary, oan have two quite different sources: first, stimuli produced by muscular activity, which I shall call *re*-afference; second, stimuli produced by external factors, which I shall call *ex*-afference. Re-afference is the necessary afferent reflexion caused by every motor impulse; ex-afference is independent of motor impulses.

Here are some examples: when I turn my eyes, the image present on the retina moves over the retina. The stimuli so produced in the optic nerve constitute a re-afference, for this is the necessary result of my eye movement. If I shake my head, a re-afference necessarily is produced by the labyrinth. If, on the other hand, I stand on a railway platform looking straight at a train when it starts to move, the moving image on the retina of my unmoving eye produces an ex-afference; likewise, when I lie in a tossing ship, the impulses of my labyrinth will constitute an ex-afference. If I shake the branch of a tree, various receptors of my skin and joints produce a re-afference, but if I place my hand on a branch shaken by the wind, the stimuli of the same receptors produce an ex-afference. We can see that this distinction has nothing to do with the difference between the so called proprio- and extero-receptors. The *same* receptor can serve both the re- and the ex-afference. The CNS, must, however, possess the ability to distinguish one from the other. This distinction is indispensable for every organism, since it must correctly perceive its environment at rest and in movement, and stimuli resulting from its own movements must not be interpreted as movements of the environment. I want to describe experiments which show how the CNS distinguishes between ex-afference and re-afference.

When one rotates a striped cylinder around a quietly sitting insect, for instance the fly Eristalis, the animal turns itself in the same sense (Figure 1a). This is a well-known optomotor-"reflex."

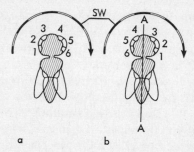

FIGURE 1.   Insect (Eristalis) in striped cylinder (SW), L, R = left, right eyes; a = head in normal, b = in turned position.

As soon as the animal moves itself, for instance, "spontaneously" (or stimulated by a smell), one observes that it turns itself unhindered by the stripes of the stationary cylinder. We must ask ourselves why the animal at every turn is not turned back by his optomotor-"reflex," since the movement of the image on the retina is the same as in the first case, when the cylinder moved and the animal was stationary. A possible answer according to the reflex-theory is that in locomotion the optomotor-"reflex" is inhibited or "blocked." But we shall see that this answer is incorrect. It is possible, as has been shown by my colleague Mittelstaedt, to turn the head of the insect through 180° about the long axis (Figure 1b A–A); then the head is fixed to the thorax, so that the two eyes are effectively interchanged and the order of the visual elements is reversed. The unmoving animal now responds, when the cylinder turns to the right, by turning itself to the left, as is to be expected from the reversed position of the eyes. If it is indeed the case that in spontaneous (or otherwise caused) locomotion the optomotor-reflex is "blocked," the animal should move *un*hindered in the stationary cylinder. But the opposite is the case; once the insect begins to move, it spins rapidly to right or left in small circles until it is exhausted. We have observed the same behaviour with fishes, whose eyes have been turned 180° about the optic axis. But we have found this behaviour only in patterned optical surroundings; in optically homogeneous surroundings the animal moves normally. This indicates that the optomotor-"reflex" is not "blocked" in locomotion, but on the contrary, the associated re-afference plays an important role. Exactly what that role is will be made clearer by the next example.

If a vertebrate is turned over on its side by external forces, the well-known righting "reflexes" are initiated by the ex-afference of the labyrinth. But, just as in my first example, every animal is able to take up any position without righting reflexes being produced by the re-afference of the labyrinth. Again, it has been believed that the reflexes were "blocked" during position changing; and, again, we can show that this is not the case.

The righting reflexes, as is well-known, are released by the statoliths in the labyrinths, which, when the head is tilted, produce a shearing force on the underlying sensory organ, as we have found in fishes. One can increase this mechanical force which the statoliths exert on the sense organs, through the addition of a constant centrifugal force. We have built for this purpose a small revolving laboratory, capable of more than doubling the gravitational force. In this manner the statolith is made heavier, and the corresponding shearing stimuli produced by every tilting of the head are quantitatively increased. If one records the tilting of free swimming fish under these conditions, one finds that the degree of tilting becomes proportionally less, the heavier the statoliths are made. (For the method of measurement see v. Holst and Mittelstaedt, 1950.) If the statoliths are removed, then the behaviour of the fish is the same under normal and centrifugal conditions. We see, therefore, that the re-afference of the labyrinth is not "blocked," but has a quantitative effect upon the *degree* of tilting, and, indeed, the greater the re-afference, the smaller the degree of the movement. One can say that the CNS "measures" the degree of movement by the magnitude of the re-afference thereby released.

Thus we have learned two facts: if the form of the re-afference is reversed, as in the first example, then the initiated movement is . increased progressively. Secondly, if the re-afference keeps its normal form but is increased, as in the second example, the initiated movement is correspondingly decreased. These facts allow us to formulate a hypothesis about the mechanism here involved. We shall propose that the efference leaves an "image" of itself somewhere in the CNS, to which the re-afference of this movement compares as the negative of a photograph compares to its print; so that, when superimposed, the image disappears. Figure 2 illustrates this

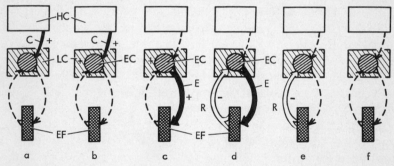

FIGURE 2.   Illustration of the re-afference principle; see explanation in text.

in a number of subsequent steps. A motor impulse, a "command" C (Figure 2a), from a higher centre HC causes a specific activation in a lower centre LC (Figure 2b), which is the stimulus-situation giving rise to a specific efference E (Figure 2c) to the effector EF (that is, a muscle, a joint, or the whole organism). This central stimulus situation, the "image" of the efference, may be called "efference copy," EC. The effector, activated by the efference, produces a re-afference R, which returns to the lower centre, nullifying the efference copy by superposition (Figure 2d-f). Because of the complementary action of these two components we can arbitrarily designate the whole efferent part of this process as plus (+, dark coloured) and the afferent part as minus (−, white coloured). When the efference copy and the re-afference exactly compensate one another, nothing further happens. When, however, the afference is too small or lacking, then a + difference will remain or when the re-afference is too great, a − difference will remain. This difference will have definite effects, according to the particular organisation of the system. The difference can either influence the movement itself, or for instance, ascend to a higher centre and produce a perception.

Let us first consider the simple situation of Figure 2. The initiated movement will continue, until the re-afference exactly nullifies the efference copy. Then we must predict the following: first, if through external influence the re-afference is increased, then the initiated movement will end prematurely. We have already seen that this is the case in the fish labyrinth experiment with the centrifuge. Secondly (Figure 3a), if the re-afference is inverted, that is changed

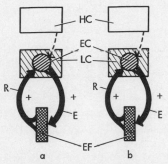

FIGURE 3. Illustration of the experiment with the eyes in turned position (Figure 1); see explanation in text.

from − to +, there will be nullification, but summation (Figure 3b) and the movement will progressively increase, as we have already seen in the experiment with the inverted eyes.[1] Thirdly (Figure 4), in the case where the re-afference is lacking (for instance, due to the destruction of the afferent pathways) the initiated movement will not be increased, as in the second case, but will continue until something else limits it. This behaviour occurs widely and can be seen particularly well in fish without labyrinths in optically homogeneous surroundings. Every turning or tilt leads to circling or somersaulting. Also, in the human disease Tabes dor-

[1] This is the so called "positive feed-back."

salis, where the dorsal roots are destroyed, the well-known exaggerated, ataxic movements of the limbs indicate that the same mechanism is involved. Therefore, contrary to the chain-reflex theory, the stimulus, originating with every movement, that is, the re-afference, produces not an augmenting, excitatory, but a *limiting*, effect on the movement. Only those forms of locomotion, such as the swimming of fish, which do not require a constant adjustment to the surrounding medium, proceed just as before after de-afferentation. These movements are automatically co-ordinated in the CNS and therefore require no limiting re-afference (v. Holst, Lissmann).

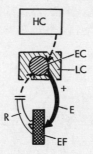

Figure 4. Illustration of the experiment with interrupted afference; see explanation in text.

With this simple scheme we are able to understand a number of previously unexplained types of behaviour. The most hypothetical part of this theory is the postulated efference copy: this "image" in the CNS, produced by the "command" and matched by the re-afference. I am going to present direct proof of the existence of this phenomenon. For this purpose I choose two human examples, in which the difference between the efference copy and re-afference is transmitted to a higher centre and produces a perception. My first example is concerned with the already mentioned human eye movement.

A re-afference from the actively moving eye can have two sources: firstly, movement of the image across the retina and secondly, impulses from the sensory cells of the eye muscles. The former results in a conscious perception; the latter is of no importance for the following consideration. Consider my eye mechanically fixed and the muscle receptors narcotised (Figure 5a). When I want to turn my eye to the right, an efference E and, according to the theory, an efference-copy EC is produced, but the immovable eye does not produce any re-afference. The efference-copy will not be nullified, but transmitted to higher centers and could produce a perception. tI is possible to predict the exact form of this perception (v. Holst and Mittelstaedt, 1950). The perception if I want to turn my eye to the right, must be that "the sur-

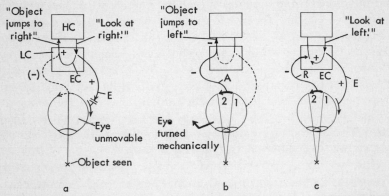

FIGURE 5. Illustration of the experiments with human eye; explanation in text (for the letters compare the text of Figure 2).

roundings have jumped to the right." This is indeed the case! It has been known for many years from people with paralysed eye muscles and it has been established exactly from the experiments of Kornmuller on himself that every intended but unfulfilled eye movement results in the perception of a quantitative movement of the surroundings in the same direction. Since here *nothing* happens on the afferent pathways, this false perception *can* only result from the activity, originated by the intention of the eye movement, being returned to higher centres. This is another way of saying that the unmatched efference-copy causes the perception.

Now, we make a simple experiment and turn the paralysed eye mechanically to the right (Figure 5b). In this case both the motor intention and also the efference-copy are lacking, but the image moves across the retina and afference A is transmitted, unmatched by an efference-copy, to higher centres and produces, as is known, the perception that "the surroundings move to the left." This is also a false perception. If now we combine the first case with the second, that is, if my eye is moved mechanically at the same time I intend this movement—which is the same as *voluntarily* moving a *normal* eye—then in fact these two complementary effects just mentioned are produced: firstly, the perception of the returning "command" causing a jump of the surroundings to the right and, secondly, an image-motion on the retina producing a jump of the surroundings in the opposite direction. These two phenomena, the efference-copy and the re-afference, now compensate each other (Figure 5c); and as a result *no moving* of the surroundings is perceived. The surroundings appear stationary during this normal eye movement, and *this* perception is *physically correct*. As we have already seen, the correct perception results from two opposite and false perceptions which cancel each other. Thus, we understand a phenomenon with which Psychology has been concerned for many years, that is, the perception of the surroundings as nearly stationary during eye movements ("Raumkonstanz").

Now we come to the second example, visual accommodation. The eye is focussed for distant vision when at rest, since the elastic lens is flattened by its zonal fibres. For near-accommodation a circular muscle, working against these fibres, allows the lens to round up. We should also like to apply our theory to this system. If the accommodation apparatus is narcotised (for instance by atrophine), that is, the eye is permanently accommodated for distant vision, then an intention for near-accommodation will start a motor-impulse, which cannot be nullified by any re-afference and, therefore, must return to a higher centre, where it can produce a perception. This is indeed the case. All objects in the visual field become small, and this false perception is called "micropsia." The same phenomenon must exist with a normal eye, if we imprint an after-image of a distant cross on the retina and then look upon a near surface. Since the after-image remains the same size and sharpness on the retina, it must appear very small on the near surface, because again only the "command" for accommodation returns to the centre of perception. This is also the case, as one can easily convince oneself. These false perceptions appear, although the *peripheral stimulus-situation* is *un*altered. If, on the contrary, the *accommodation* of a normal eye is *un*altered, that is, if we look first at a small and then at a large cross at the *same* distance, then naturally the changed afference will be transmitted to the centre of perception and we see the second cross to be larger. Now we combine this last case with the first, that is, we observe with a *normal* eye a cross, moving from a distant point nearer to the eye. This initiates the accommodation-impulse, which returning, tells us "the cross is becoming smaller"; but at the same time the enlargement of the retinal image states, "the cross is becoming larger." The two cancel one another out, with the result that we perceive the cross to be of *constant* size. Again, the correct perception is the result of two opposite false perceptions; and, further, we come to an understanding of a phenomenon, long discussed in Psychology, the "GrössenKonstanz der Sehdinge" (Hering), which means that we see the objects to be nearly the same size irrespective of their distance from us.

I could present still further examples from man and from lower and higher animals which would show what role the re-afference plays in general in behaviour. It serves either to limit the magnitude of movement or to insure the constancy of the perceived surroundings during movement, and so makes possible the distinction between real and apparent motion of objects. The first step in both of these functional mechanisms is the comparison of the re-afference with the efference-copy.

In conclusion, permit me a few general considerations. I have attempted to show through the example of this central nervous mechanism, that it is possible in the field of the Physiology of Behaviour to avoid formulating "theories," which are only generalised descriptions of observations; rather should we follow the example of the exact sciences, namely, that a theory must exactly predict what will happen under defined conditions, so that one can by experiment verify or disprove it. Thus one avoids the error of false generalisation, which often occurs in central nervous physiology. For this reason I would like to emphasise that the principle of re-afference is only *one* of *many* central nervous mechanisms. There exists a large number of other mechanisms with other modes of function, and of these we know as yet very little. We recognise fragments of some of them and call them "reflexes"; but this term denotes fragments of very different mechanisms. I believe the whole Central-Nervous System is a "hierarchical system" of such different functional parts, a concept which you find also in Tinbergen's book "The Study of Instinct."

One final point. I have spoken of neither electrical spikes, nor nerve pathways, nor anatomical centres, in which particular functions might be localised. In the realm of behavioural analysis these things are indeed of secondary interest. The functional schemata, constructed in order to illustrate definite causal relationships, are quite abstract, although the consequences they predict are concrete and experimentally verifiable. The physiologist who fully understands such a causal system is still unable to deduce where the cell elements which perform this function are located, or how they operate. Such questions are dealt with at another level of investigation, where the electrophysiologist works and develops his own terminology. It is useful and justifiable for every level of investigation to have its own language, but we must expect, that, with a greater advancement of our knowledge, it will be easy to translate one such language into another. Until such a time, each field must develop along its own lines, unhindered by the many possibilities for misinterpretation.

Bibliography

Adrian, E. D. *The Basis of Sensation. The Action of the Sense Organs.* London: Christophers, 1928.

————. *The Physical Background of Perception.* (The Waynflete Lectures.) Oxford: Clarendon, 1947.

Bartlett, F. C. *Remembering.* Cambridge: Cambridge University Press, 1932.

Biological Clocks. Cold Spring Harbor Symposia on Quantitative Biology, XXV. Cold Spring Harbor, L.I.: Long Island Biological Association, 1960.

Boring, E. G. *Sensation and Perception in the History of Experimental Psychology.* New York: Appleton-Century, 1942.

————. "The Moon Illusion," *American Journal of Physics,* 1943, 11, 55–60.

Brady, F. B. "All-Weather Aircraft Landing," *Scientific American,* March 1964, 25.

Brown, J. L. "Sensory and Perceptual Problems in Space Flight," in *Physiological Problems in Space Exploration.* Springfield, Ill.: Charles C Thomas, 1964.

Bude, J. *Influence de relations inter-individuelles sur l'estimation de la taille.* Université Libre de Bruxelles, 1960.

Chapanis, A. "Psychology and the Instrument Panel," *Scientific American,* April 1953, 74.

Dunlap, K. *Habits: Their Making and Unmaking.* New York: Liveright, 1932.

Epstein, W., J. Park, and A. Casey. *Psychological Bulletin,* 1961, 58, 491.

Erickson, M. H. "Experimental Demonstrations of the Psycotherapy of Everyday Life," *Psychoanalytic Quarterly,* 1939, 8, 338–353.

Evans, R. *An Introduction to Color.* New York: Wiley, 1948.

Fantz, R. L. "Ontogeny of Perception," in Schrier, A. M., H. F. Harlow, and F. Stollnitz (eds.). *Behavior of Non-Human Primates,* Vol. 2. New York: Academic, 1965.

Fantz, R. L. "The Origin of Form Perception," *Scientific American,* May 1961, 66.

Frisch, Karl v. *Bees: Their Vision, Chemical Senses, and Language.* Ithaca, N.Y.: Cornell, 1950.

————. "Dialects in the Language of the Bees," *Scientific American,* August 1962, 78.

Gibson, E. J., and R. D. Walk. "The 'Visual Cliff,' " *Scientific American,* April 1960, 64.

Gilinsky, A. *American Journal of Psychology,* 1955, 68, 173.

Graham, C. H. "Visual Perception," in S. S. Stevens (ed.). *Handbook of Experimental Psychology.* New York: Wiley, 1951, Ch. 23·

Griffin, D. "The Navigation of Birds," *Scientific American,* December 1948, 18.

Hasler A. D., and J. A. Larsen. "The Homing Salmon," *Scientific American,* August 1955, 72.

Hasler, A. D., and Warren J. Wisby. "Discrimination of Stream Odors by Fishes and its Relation to Parent Stream Behavior," *The American Naturalist,* 1951, 85, 223–238.

Helmholtz, H. v. *Physiological Optics,* Vol. III, J. P. C. Southall (ed.). New York: Optical Society of America, 1925, pp. 290–292.

————. *Physiological Optics,* Vol. III. Reprinted. New York: Dover, 1962. (a)

————. "The Recent Progress of the Theory of Vision," in *Popular Scientific Lectures.* New York: Dover, 1962. (b)

Holst, E. v. "Aktive Leistungen der menschlichen Gesichtswahrnehmung," *Studium Generale,* 1947, 10, 231–243.

Holst, E. v., and H. Mittelstaedt. *Naturwissenschaften,* 1950, 464–476.

Holway, A. H., and E. G. Boring. *American Journal of Psychology,* 1940, 53, 109, 537.

Human Factors in Underseas Warfare. Washington, D.C.: National Research Council, Committee on Underseas Warfare, 1949.

Ittelson, W. H., and F. P. Kilpatrick. "Experiments in Perception," *Scientific American,* August 1951, 50.

James, W. *Principles of Psychology.* New York: Holt, 1890. Reprinted. New York: Dover, 1950.

Katz, D. *Animals and Men. Studies in Comparative Psychology.* London: Longmans, Green, 1937.

Kaufman, E. L., M. W. Lord, T. W. Reese, and J. Volkmann. "The Discrimination of Visual Number," *American Journal of Psychology,* 1949, 62, 498–525.

Kaufman, L., and I. Rock. *Science,* 1962, 136, 953.

Kersta, L. G. "Voice-Print Identification," *Nature,* 1962, 196, 1253–1257.

Kohler, I. "Experiments with Goggles," *Scientific American,* May 1962, 62.

Kolers, P. A. "The Illusion of Movement," *Scientific American,* October 1964, 98.

Leibowitz, H., and T. Hartman. "Magnitude of the Moon Illusion as a Function of the Age of the Observer," *Science,* 1959, **130**, 569.

Leibowitz, H., and M. Heisel. "L'évolution de l'illusion de Ponzo en fonction de l'âge," *Archives de Psychologie* (Geneva), 1958, **36**, 328–331.

Leuba, C. "The Use of Hypnosis for Controlling Variables in Psychological Experiments," *Journal of Abnormal Psychology,* 1941, **36**, 271–274.

Levine, K. N., J. R. Grassi, and M. J. Gerson. "Hypnotically Induced Mood Changes in the Verbal and Graphic Rorschach: A Case Study," *Rorschach Research Exchange,* 1944, **8**, 104–124.

Levine, L., I. Chein, and G. Murphy. "The Relation of the Intensity of a Need to the Amount of Perceptual Distortion: A Preliminary Report," *Journal of Psychology,* 1942, **13**, 283–293.

Lindzey, G. *Projective Techniques in Cross-Cultural Research.* New York: Appleton-Century, 1961.

Mercury Project Summary Including Results of the Fourth Manned Orbital Flight. May 1963 S.P.–45. Washington, D.C.: National Aeronautics and Space Administration.

Luckiesch, M. *Visual Illusions.* New York: Van Nostrand, 1922.

Miller, A. Thesis. Philadelphia: Pennsylvania State College, 1943.

Miller, G. A. "The Magical Number Seven, Plus or Minus Two: Some Limits on Our Capacity for Processing Information," *Psychological Review,* 1956, **63**, 81–97.

Morris, A., and E. P. Horne. *Visual Search Techniques.* Publication 712. Washington, D.C.: National Academy of Sciences, National Research Council, 1960.

Murphy, G. "The Freeing of Intelligence," *Psychological Bulletin,* 1945, **42**, 1–19.

Murray, H. A. "The Effect of Fear upon Estimates of the Maliciousness of Other Personalities," *Journal of Social Psychology,* 1933, **4**, 310–339.

Osgood, C. E. *Method and Theory in Experimental Psychology.* New York: Oxford University Press, 1953.

Neuberger, H. *General Meteorological Optics in Compendium of Meteorology.* Boston: American Meteorological Society, 1952, pp. 61–70.

Piaget, J., and M. Lambercier. *Archives Psychologie* (Geneva), 1956, **35**, 257.

Poffenberger, A. T. *Principles of Applied Psychology.* New York: Appleton-Century, 1942.

Proshansky, H. A. "A Projective Technique for the Study of Attitudes," *Journal of Abnormal Psychology*, 1943, **38**, 393–394.

Rapaport, D. *Emotions and Memory*. Baltimore: Williams and Wilkins, 1942.

Ratliff, F., and H. K. Hartline. "The Responses of *Limulus* Optic Nerve Fibers to Patterns of Illumination on the Receptor Mosaic," *Journal of General Physiology*, 1959, **42**, 1241–1255.

Renner, M. "The Contribution of the Honey Bee to the Study of the Time-Sense and Astronomical Orientation," in *Biological Clocks*. Cold Spring Harbor Symposia on Quantitative Biology, XXV. Cold Spring Harbor, L.I.: Long Island Biological Association, 1960.

Rock, I. *American Journal of Psychology*, 1956, **69**, 513.

Rock, I., and S. Ebenholtz. *Psychological Review*, 1959, **66**, 387.

Rock, I., and N. Heimer. *American Journal of Psychology*, 1957, **70**, 493.

Sanford, R. N. "The Effects of Abstinence from Food upon Imaginal Processes," *Journal of Psychology*, 1936, **2**, 129–136.

———. "The Effects of Abstinence from Food upon Imaginal Processes: A Further Experiment," *Journal of Psychology*, 1937, **3**, 145–159.

Sauer, E. G. F. "Celestial Navigation by Birds," *Scientific American*, August 1958, 42.

Sauer, E. G. F., and E. M. Sauer. "Star Navigation of Nocturnal Migrating Birds," in *Biological Clocks*. Cold Spring Harbor Symposia on Quantitative Biology, XXV. Cold Spring Harbor, L.I.: Long Island Biological Association, 1960.

Schur, E. *Psychologische Forschung*, 1925, **7**, 40.

Sinaiko, H. W. *Selected Papers on Human Factors in the Design and Use of Control Systems*. New York: Dover, 1961.

Taylor, D. E., and E. G. Boring. *American Journal of Psychology*, 1942, **55**, 189.

Thouless, R. H. "Phenomenal Regression to the 'Real' Object. I, II," *British Journal of Psychology*, 1931, **21**, 339–359; **22**, 1–30.

———. *British Journal of Psychology*, 1932, **22**, 216.

Tinbergen, N. *The Study of Instinct*. London: Oxford, 1951.

Wald, G. "Eye and Camera," *Scientific American*, August 1950, 2.

Woodworth, R. S., and M. R. Sheehan. *Contemporary Schools of Psychology*. New York: Ronald, 1964.

Woodworth, R. S., and H. Schlosberg. *Experimental Psychology*, Second Edition. New York: Holt, 1954.

Zeigler, H. P., and H. Leibowitz. "A Methodological Study of Shape Constancy in the Rhesus Monkey," *Journal of Comparative and Physiological Psychology*, 1958, **51**, 155–160.

Index

Aberrations of the eye, 57–60
Adaptation to disarranged eye-hand
   coordination, 91–95; *see also*
   Prism adaptation
Adaptation to the perceptual world,
   3–9
Attention, 28–34
  in advertising, 33
  disorders of, 28–29, 33–34
  effect of experience, 29
  effect of motivation, 29
  and interpersonal relations 33
  span of, 29–30
Attitudes, effect on descriptions of pictures, 96–104

Brightness
  constancy, 6–7, 67–69
  contrast, 57–58

Central nervous system, relation to
   peripheral organs, 160–70
Clues: *see* Cues
Color; *see also* Hue
  constancy, 7–8, 67, 69
  fringes, 59
  memory for, 8
Communication
  dances in bees, 10–12
  in war, 155–58

Constancy; *see also* Brightness; Color;
   Position constancy; Raumkonstanz; Shape constancy; Size
  in animals, 9
  explanation of, 8, 69–71, 80
  importance of, 9, 76, 84–85
Context, 5, 7, 8, 69, 71, 74, 78–79, 135
Cues
  gravitational, 30–32
  visual, 30–32, 70, 71, 79, 80, 85, 105

Depth perception, 14–15
Distance perception, 72–79, 84, 121–
   22, 135–40
Distorted room, 39–40, 105–19

Efference copy, 164–66, 168
Emmert's law, 73, 140
Engineering psychology, 53
Euclid's rule, 72, 73, 75, 77
Evolution, role of vision in, 14, 16–17
Exafference, 62, 92, 161–62

Face recognition, 23–24
Fighting in the dark, 152–54
Flying saucers, 36–37

Gestalt psychology, 46, 73, 82–83
Grössen Konstanz, 169; *see also* Size,
   constancy

Habits, 33–34
Honi phenomenon, 39–40, 105–19
Hue, 67, 69; *see also* Color
Human engineering, 53, 155
Human factors, 53, 55
Hypnosis, 38–39
  effect of attitudes on, 96–104

Illusions, 42–49, 80–81
  apparent motion, 46
  importance of, 42, 48–49
  moon, 47–48, 79, 120–44
  of Ponzo, 44–45, 47
  relation to experience, 42–45
Infant vision, 14–16
Innate behavior, 10–17, 83
Inner clock, 13; *see also* Time sense
Insignia, 151–52
Instinctive behavior: *see* Innate behavior
Inverted retinal image, 21–22, 72, 92

Learning process in perception, 18–27, 84
  role of activity in, 22–23, 91–95
  significance of, 26

Man-machine relationship, 51–55, 144–59
Migration of animals, 13–14, 19–21
Moon illusion, 47–48, 79, 120–44
Motion, 46, 61
Motivation and perception, 35–41, 105–19
Movement perception, 20
"Mystery" house, 30–32

Nervous system
  activation of individual fibers, 56–58
  inhibition in, 57–58
  interaction in, 57–60

Optical image in eye, 3–4, 36, 57–60
Optomotor reflex, 61, 162–63
Organism, contribution to perception, 6

Pattern vision in infants, 15–16
Perception; *see also* Brightness; Color; Hue; Shape constancy; Size
  definition of, vii

purpose of, 3
relation to general psychology, viii
scope of, vii–viii
in space, 52
in technology, 50–55, 144–59
Perceptual
  distortion, 39–41, 105–19
  learning, 20–23
    role of activity in, 23, 59, 61–63
  selectivity, 28–34
Ponzo illusion
  basis of, 44–45
  development in children, 45
Position constancy, 62; *see also* Raumkonstanz
Prism adaptation, 22–23; *see also* Adaptation to disarranged eye-hand coordination
Projective techniques, 37–38
Psychophysics and radar engineering, 149–51

Radar screen, eyes and, 148–49
Raumkonstanz, 168; *see also* Position constancy
Reaction time, 50–51
Reafference, 62, 92, 95, 161, 166–69
Reduction, 69, 71–72, 77
  of context, 70–72
  screen, 5, 71–72
  tunnel, 77
Regression, 69
Regression toward the real object, 71
Relearning, role of activity in, 22–23
Releasers, 12–13
Reliability of witnesses, 37
Retinal image, 3–4, 8, 9, 21–22, 44–45, 57–58, 63, 68, 70, 78, 83–84
Rorschach test, 37

Shape constancy, 8–9, 67–68; *see also* Regression toward the real object
Size
  biological use of, 84–85
  constancy, 4–6, 67–68, 70–73, 75–76, 86–89; *see also* Grössen Konstanz
  effect of experience on, 5–6, 83–84, 86–91

Size (*Continued*)
  importance of, 4
  influence of prestige on, 38
  mechanisms, 5–6
  perceived, 7, 67, 72–79, 135–37
  relation to Ponzo illusion, 44–45, 47
Speech, packaging of, 158–59

Time sense, 18–19; *see also* Inner clock

Transactional viewpoint in perception, 118

Unbewusster Schluss, 80
Unconscious inference, 80

Visual cliff, 14–15
Voice prints, 24
Voice recognition, 24–26